FASHION SEWING

INTRODUCTORY TECHNIQUES

Connie Amaden-Crawford

Fairchild Books

An imprint of Bloomsbury Publishing Plc

50 Bedford Square	1385 Broadway
London	New York
WC1B 3DP	NY 10018
UK	USA

www.bloomsbury.com

Bloomsbury is a registered trade mark of
Bloomsbury Publishing Plc.

First published 2014

© Bloomsbury Publishing Plc, 2014

British Library Cataloguing-in-Publication Data
A catalogue record for this book is available
from the British Library.

ISBN: PB: 978-1-4725-2945-9

Design by Megan Trudell
Printed and bound in China

PREFACE

Fashion Sewing: Introductory Techniques is written for all those with an interest in constructing garments, whether you are a beginner or have sewing experience. When learning how to sew, it is important to understand how to assemble a garment and how to sew each and every item within the garment.

The easy-to-read text is accompanied by step-by-step sewing instructions and illustrations. It guides beginners and more seasoned sewers through all the basic and intermediate skills required to sew garments from a pattern. You will then be able to create simple and more complex fashionable, professional-looking garments.

The first chapter of the book will enable you to set up your sewing workshop. It outlines all the main types of sewing machine and overlocker, as well as general sewing supplies and equipment. Chapter 2 is an introduction to textiles and includes information on the newest fibres and blends, with a section on eco-friendly fibres. Chapter 3 is a useful resource for those who are interested in sewing for others as well as themselves, offering information on taking measurements and typical size charts in commercial patterns. The fitting techniques in Chapter 4 illustrate the method of fitting a design as followed in the fashion industry. Chapters 5 through to 8 provide basic construction techniques from stitches and seams to hems and closures.

This text promises to be an excellent resource for anyone who desires to learn more about fashion sewing. Many years of experience in fashion design rooms, production rooms and college classrooms have taught me that solid, competent sewing skills result in good design. It is my sincere wish that the skills learned through study of this text will provide a solid foundation for success in fashion sewing.

CONTENTS

CHAPTER
1

GETTING STARTED

- Setting up your Workshop

- Sewing Machines

- Overlockers

- Sewing Equipment and Tools

- Pressing Equipment and Tools

- Pressing Methods

SETTING UP
YOUR WORKSHOP

When setting up your workshop, take the time to organize all equipment and ensure that it is in working order and ready for use. A pleasant, enjoyable place to sew should be well lit: good-quality lighting in a sewing area is essential. Although daylight is ideal, there are many high-intensity and 'daylight' lamps available.

The cutting surface should be large enough to cut the sewing projects. The cutting surface must be firm to prevent the fabric from shifting. The ironing board and iron should be set up near the sewing machine. A full-length mirror is helpful for checking the fit and appearance of the garment.

A variety of sewing tools, notions, and supplies are needed for any sewing project. All sewing-related items should be kept in specific areas, special cabinets or containers for ease of access and use. The following supplies and equipment, discussed in detail later in this chapter, should be assembled and kept in the sewing area:

- Sewing machine
- Iron and ironing board
- Thread
- Tape measure
- Pins and needles
- Scissors
- Nippers
- Rotary cutters (optional)
- Metre rule
- Miscellaneous supplies

STUDIO TIP

Use a fishing tackle box to keep sewing tools together. Tackle boxes are available in a variety of sizes and configurations, with compartments to hold all the tools in a convenient space. It is portable and easy to set up each time you sew.

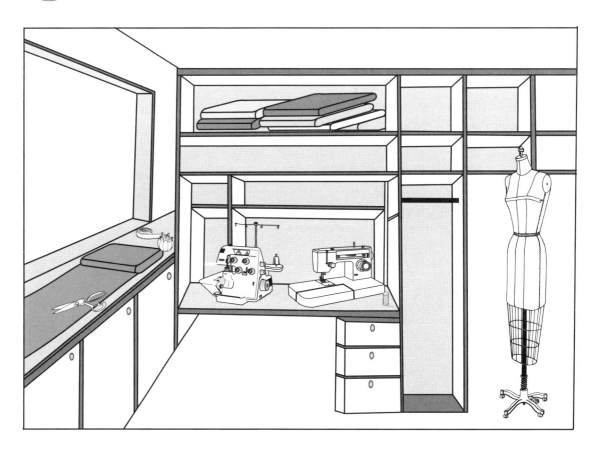

SEWING MACHINES

A sewing machine uses a needle and rotary hook to interlock threads above (upper thread) and below (bobbin thread) a piece of fabric to produce a stitch. These stitches can be designed to simply lock two fabrics together, encase the raw edges of a seam or decorate fabric with a specific pattern. Sewing machine models contain single or multiple stitch functions.

Selecting a sewing machine can be a daunting task. From older models with basic functions to top-of-the-line models with internal computers and a variety of features, a profusion of sewing machine models is available on the market today. Choose a machine that is suitable for the planned usage. An artistic home sewer might want a machine with many creative stitch functions, whereas a garment factory would select a machine with basic stitch functions and a stronger motor for faster sewing speeds. To help you select a machine and simplify the decision process, this chapter presents the basic attributes of machine types and uses. If possible, it is best to try a number of machines before making a final decision.

MACHINE CLASSIFICATIONS

Sewing machines can be divided into two categories – household and industrial – both with an array of model types. However, the difference is the intended use. Industrial machines are designed for prolonged, continuous use at high speeds. These machines are designed for highly repetitive sewing tasks. Household machines operate at much slower stitching speeds and include a greater number of functions because they are intended to be general-purpose machines, suitable for clothing repair and construction, quilting and crafts.

HOUSEHOLD MACHINES

A good household sewing machine should operate smoothly, producing neat, uniform stitches. These are designed to be versatile machines on which the user can easily and quickly switch among functions. Basic sewing machines usually offer straight stitch (forward and reverse), zigzag stitch, adjustable stitch widths and lengths and a buttonhole function. Blind hem and stretch blind hem stitches are also commonly available on basic machines.

New machine models range hugely in price from £60 to £8,000. With increasing price tends to come increasing complexity and versatility. Household machines can be either completely mechanical or computerized. Mechanical machines tend to be less expensive and less versatile, but long-lived. Computerized machines tend to be very versatile, more expensive, and sometimes have 'sewing advisory' functions to help select a suitable stitch and presser foot combination. In the past, all machines used a mechanical gear train to transmit power from the motor to the working parts of a machine. Today, with both mechanical and computerized models available, buttons or a touch screen are usually used to select stitch settings. More expensive machines generally have a greater number of utility and decorative stitches and often increased ease of use.

Engineering details are also a consideration. A machine with a series-wound motor may stall or not produce much force on the needle when sewing at slow speeds. Servo and stepper motors, generally found in computerized or electronic machines, produce full force even at the slowest stitching speeds; an advantage when working with some fabrics. The choice of a mechanical or computerized machine generally depends on budget considerations and desire for ease of use or versatility. A used, well-maintained machine, often available from sewing machine centres that sell new machines, may fit into your budget.

INDUSTRIAL MACHINES

All the components of an industrial machine are designed for efficient garment construction, saving time and money. The actual machine, called the 'machine head', is configured with a specific stitch for a specific step and can be sized and shaped accordingly. It also typically contains a bobbin system that winds extra bobbins during stitching. The machine head is set into a table that houses a separate clutch motor, a pedal, a thread stand, an automatic lubrication system, a pedal brake that lifts the machine needle when desired, and a knee lift that raises the presser foot so hands can remain free to manipulate the fabric. Industrial machines are typically customized for a single purpose, such as straight stitching, special seams, buttonholes, zips and bias binding, and they might be specialized for different materials being used. These various applications often use specially made presser feet to sew a specific task.

BASIC MACHINE FUNCTIONS NECESSARY FOR FASHION SEWING

(Listed in order of importance)
- Straight stitch
- Variable stitch length and width
- Variable needle positions
- Zigzag stitch and variations
- Buttonhole (single and multiple styles)
- Miscellaneous utility stitches: blind hem stitch, edge-finishing stitch and stretch stitch

USEFUL FEATURES

Advances in engineering and technology continue to provide greater efficiency and precision in machine sewing. Some helpful features are listed as follows:
- Automatic needle threading: a device that hooks the thread through the needle eye
- Automatic bobbin thread raising when bobbin is inserted
- Automatic presser foot lifter
- Automatic thread tensioning
- Automatic stitch length regulation for free motion work (embroidery or quilting)
- Automatic jump stitch cutter that finishes and cuts the thread between embroidery sections of the same colour

- Automatic 'tie off', which begins and ends a seam with locking stitches
- Thread cutter: a function that automatically cuts the thread at the end of the seam
- Needle camera: a small camera that displays the exact needle position on a display screen
- Speed control: adjusts the maximum speed allowed
- Stitch memory: allows stitch configurations and combinations to be stored for later use; often used for making identical buttonholes as well as for decorative stitching
- Needle up/down: sets the needle to stop automatically in the up or down position, making tasks like pivoting at the end of a seam easier
- Multidirectional stitching, including sewing sideways
- Larger bobbin capacity
- Sensor that warns when bobbin thread is low or out of thread
- Automatic buttonhole sizing sensors
- Stitching advisor: suggests machine settings and presser feet for particular stitches
- Large harp: a larger area to the right of the presser foot; of special interest to machine quilters and those embroidering on large projects
- Function for personal decorative and creative stitches, including geometric, floral and novelty stitches
- Improved lighting, such as halogen or LED for better colour balance and brightness, which produce bright light with little heat and larger areas of illumination
- Interactive touch screens

Some features, such as automatic thread trimming, knee lifts, or needle up/down can help you sew more efficiently. Be aware that new technology can sometimes complicate machine operations or require more frequent repair. Features that sometimes help new sewers can annoy more experienced sewers who want to be able to control fabric feeding, needle positioning, back stitching and other details.

MACHINE STYLES

Console machines are designed to set into a table, creating a large, flat area for sewing – especially useful for large projects. Portable machines can be set up on any tabletop and thus travel well for classes and may be easily stored. Portable machines typically offer a 'free arm' option that some people find useful. Combination embroidery/ sewing machines usually have at least two extensions to the machine bed for regular sewing and for embroidery.

Sewing machines are available in two bobbin designs – case or top-loading. In the case style machine, the bobbin is loaded into a bobbin case that is then latched into a compartment beneath the needle plate. Drop-in bobbins are simply placed into a compartment under the needle plate, making it easier to change bobbins in a console style machine. Both designs are commonly available and have positive and negative attributes, so the choice is left to personal preference.

Bernina Activa 210 basic computerized machine

Currently, many household machines are marketed for specific styles and types of sewing, although most have multiple stitch and feature options.

Basic Household Machines (£50–£650)

Designed for mending, alterations, home decoration sewing, and beginner to basic sewing, these are usually portable machines and offer basic utility stitches. This category includes mechanical and computerized styles; some include some decorative stitch functions and perhaps some features like automatic needle threading. Computerized machines may be less expensive than a fully mechanical machine.

TABLE 1.1 Basic Household Machines

BRAND	MODEL
Bernina	Bernette series, Activa series, Classic series, Series 2, Series 3
Brother	L14, LX17, LX25, XR27NT, XR37NT
Elna	Sew Fun, eXplore 220/240, eXplore 320/340
Husqvarna Viking	Emerald 116, Emerald 118
Janome	J3-24, 525S, 2522LE (My Style 22), CXL301, XL 601, FM725 Embellisher, Jem Platinum 760 Compact
Pfaff	Hobby Line series, Select Line series
Singer	Inspiration series, Tradition series, 1507, 2273, 2662, 8280

Fashion and Hobby Sewing Machines (£200-£2000)

These machines offer multiple stitch options, including utility and decorative stitches, often customized for various facets of hobby sewing, such as fashion sewing, heirloom sewing, quilting, home decoration and crafts.

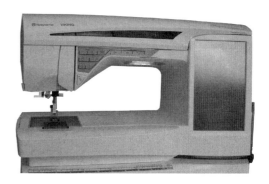

Viking Designer Diamond

TABLE 1.2 Fashion and Hobby Sewing Machines

BRAND	MODEL
Bernina	5 series
Brother	Innovis series
Elna	eXperience series
Husqvarna Viking	Emerald series, Tribute series
Janome	DKS30, TXL607, 1600PQC
Pfaff	Smarter, Expression series
Singer	Confidence series

High Fashion and Artistic Sewing Machines (£500-£8000)

For serious fabric artists and advanced fashion sewing, these computerized machines have multiple stitch functions and many decorative stitches. Most models include a number of recent innovations such as needle threading, thread cutting, stitch memory and sensors. Models in the higher price ranges are usually embroidery machines; some also interface with standard computers. Software for embroidery may also be included or available separately.

TABLE 1.3 High Fashion and Artistic Sewing Machines

BRAND	MODEL
Bernina	7 series, 8 series
Brother	Innovis series
Elna	Excellence series
Husqvarna Viking	Sapphire series, Designer series
Janome	Memory Craft series
Pfaff	Performance series, Ambition series
Singer	Quantum Stylist, Futura

Small Business/Industry Sewing, Embroidery-only Machines (£650–£6500)

A number of manufacturers offer embroidery machines without sewing machine functions. Many home sewing enthusiasts who have combination embroidery/sewing machines tend to work on a second sewing machine and use the combination machine for embroidering. Recognizing this, manufacturers have brought out single-needle, embroidery-only machines and smaller versions of multi-needle industrial embroidery machines.

TABLE 1.4 Small Business/Industry Sewing, Embroidery-only Machines

BRAND	MODEL
Bernina	Bernette 340 Deco
Brother	Innov-is 750E, Innov-is V3, PR650e 6 Needle, PR1000e 10 Needle
Elna	8300
Janome	Memory Craft 11000SE, Horizon Memory Craft 12000

Small Business/Industry Sewing Machines (£450–£6500)

Blurring the line between household and industrial machines is a group of machines meant for much heavier use than household machines, but that are generally portable or luggable and not quite as fast as standard industrial machines. For the most part, these machines generally provide utility stitches. Knee-operated presser foot lifters are common.

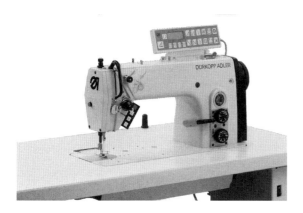

Durkopp Adler industrial machine

TABLE 1.5 Small Business/Industry Sewing Machines

BRAND	MODEL
Bernina	950 (a machine with utility and decorative stitches, including buttonholes)
Brother	S-1110A-3, S6200-403, S7200C-403, S7220B
Durkopp Adler	171-141621, 175-141621, 176-141621
Janome	1600 series
Singer	4423 Heavy Duty

Identifying Parts on the Sewing Machine

The principal parts of an average sewing machine are illustrated as follows. Specific models may differ slightly; however, all machines, whether entry level or top-of-the-range computerized, will have the same basic elements. Learn to operate the machine more efficiently by becoming familiar with the parts of a basic sewing machine and their use.

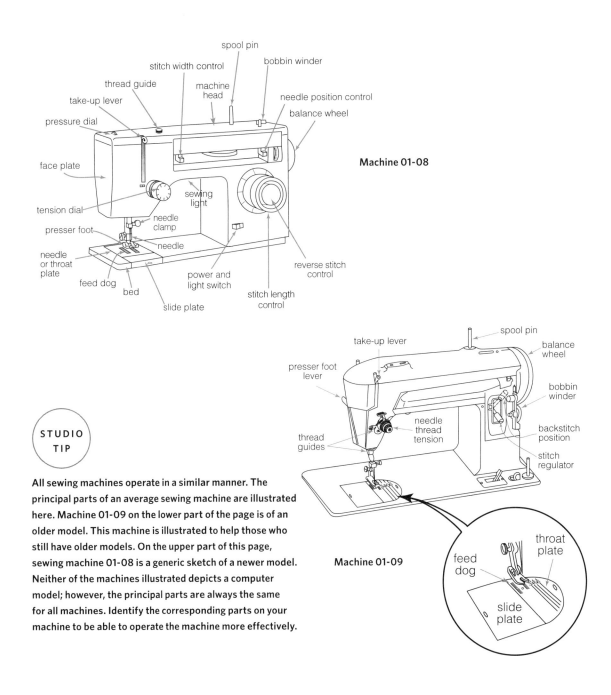

Machine 01-08

Machine 01-09

STUDIO TIP

All sewing machines operate in a similar manner. The principal parts of an average sewing machine are illustrated here. Machine 01-09 on the lower part of the page is of an older model. This machine is illustrated to help those who still have older models. On the upper part of this page, sewing machine 01-08 is a generic sketch of a newer model. Neither of the machines illustrated depicts a computer model; however, the principal parts are always the same for all machines. Identify the corresponding parts on your machine to be able to operate the machine more effectively.

Threading a Front-mounted Sewing Machine

Threading a machine involves three operations: (1) winding the bobbin, (2) threading the bobbin case, and (3) threading the machine. The following instructions illustrate the threading of an average front-mounted sewing machine. However, remember to refer to the instruction book accompanying your machine.

1 Raise the take-up lever and needle to their highest position, using the balance wheel. Raise the presser foot. Place a spool of thread on the spindle holder.

2 Lead the thread across the top of the machine into the first thread guide hook.

3 Guide the thread down to the right of the tension disk.

4 Guide the thread around the tension disk, making sure the thread falls between the two tension disks.

5 Continue around the tension disk and lead the thread into and under the tension spring lever.

6 Guide the thread back up and through the hole of the take-up lever, from right to left.

7 Lead the thread down and through the thread guides.

8 Guide the thread into the clamp near the needle holder.

9 Guide the thread through the eye of the needle. (Refer to Threading a Machine Needle later in this chapter.)

STUDIO TIPS

- If the sewing machine is incorrectly threaded, the thread of the stitch will loop on the bottom layer of fabric, the machine will skip stitches, or the needle will unthread after you sew a few stitches.
- Raising the presser foot opens the tension disks and allows the thread to enter between them.
- Some thread spools have a small nick to allow the thread end to be stored neatly. Place the nick so it is on the upper side when the spool is on the pin; this will keep the thread from accidentally catching in the nick and causing sewing problems.

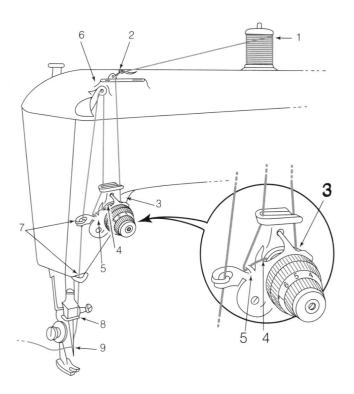

Threading a Side-mounted Machine

Many industrial machines are threaded with this side-mounted style. The principal parts are the same; however, the side tension disk parts on this model could be confusing to a beginner. Follow the diagram on this page to learn to operate this side-mounted style.

1   Raise the take-up lever and needle to their highest position, using the balance wheel. Place a spool of thread on the spindle holder. Leading the thread across the top to the first thread guide, thread this guide as illustrated.

2   Continue the thread across the top of the machine into the second thread guide.

3   Guide the thread down the beginning of the tubing channel.

4   Continue to lead the thread through the tubing channel.

5   Guide the thread around the tension disk, making sure the thread falls between the two disks. Then take the thread up and over the take-up hook.

6   Lead the thread under the take-up spring.

7   Continue to guide the thread up and through the slot of the take-up disks.

8   Pass the thread down and through the thread guides.

9   Lead the thread into the clamp near the needle holder.

10   Guide the thread through the eye of the needle. (Refer to Threading a Machine Needle later in this chapter.)

industrial version of
a side-mounted machine

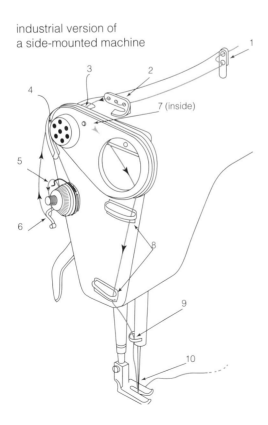

STUDIO TIP

If the sewing machine is incorrectly threaded, the thread of the stitch will loop on the bottom layer of fabric, the machine will skip stitches, or the needle will unthread after you sew a few stitches.

OTHER INDUSTRIAL MACHINES:
Front-mounted industrial machines are similar to the illustration on page 15. Use those directions as a guide in the threading of the front-mounted machine.

Threading a Machine Needle

Depending on the sewing machine, the thread could pass through the eye of the needle in one of the following three directions:

1 Front to back   **2** Right to left   **3** Left to right

STUDIO TIP If the needle thread is inserted in the wrong direction, it will unthread, or the top thread will skip stitches, or both.

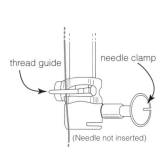

thread guide   needle clamp

(Needle not inserted)

front to back

right to left

left to right

Winding a Bobbin

Many machines have the conventional bobbin winder on the right-hand side. Others might have a bobbin that can be wound in place. Refer to the instruction book accompanying your machine. Here are the basic steps for most machines:

1 Place an empty bobbin on the bobbin winder.

2 Place a spool of thread on the spool pin.

3 Place the thread through the thread guide.

4 Continue to lead the thread from the guide to the empty bobbin. Wind the thread by hand around the bobbin three times.

5 Loosen the hand wheel tension to stop the movement of the needle. Push the drive mechanism toward the bobbin and the bobbin winder against the balance wheel (or vice versa on some machines).

6 Run the machine to wind the bobbin. Most will automatically stop winding when the bobbin fills.

7 Clip the thread and remove the bobbin from the winder. Tighten the hand wheel once again.

STUDIO TIP Not all bobbins are the same and the machine will sew poorly (if it sews at all) if you put the wrong bobbin into it. Use only the bobbins recommended by your machine's manual.

FOR INDUSTRIAL MACHINES:
To ensure that the needle does not break, make sure the presser foot is in the down position. The needle continues to go up and down. This allows a second bobbin to be winding during the sewing process.

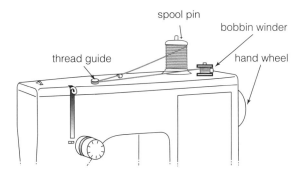

spool pin
bobbin winder
thread guide
hand wheel

Threading a Bobbin Case

Before threading the bobbin case, refer to the instruction book accompanying the machine. Some machines have a drop-in bobbin; the bobbin case remains in the machine and only the bobbin is inserted into the machine. The more common system requires inserting the filled bobbin into a removable bobbin case; the bobbin and case are then inserted into the machine at the same time.

1 Place the bobbin into the bobbin case so that the bobbin thread is in a clockwise direction. If you're looking from the side of the bobbin as you're inserting it, the thread will form the shape of a number nine.

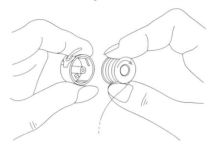

2 Lead the bobbin thread into the slot (A) and under the tension spring.

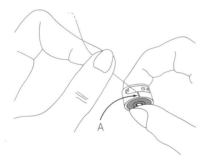

3 Continue to pull the thread around and into the notch (B, C) at the end of the spring. Leave about 7–8cm of thread hanging from the bobbin case.

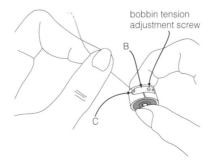

bobbin tension adjustment screw

Placing a Bobbin with a Separate Bobbin Case

1 Hold the bobbin case latch and position the bobbin case onto the stud of the machine.

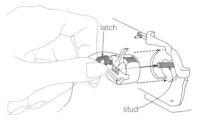

latch

stud

2 Release the latch and push the bobbin case into the machine until you hear the bobbin case click into place.

3 To remove the bobbin case, grasp the latch and pull it away from the bobbin case; pull the bobbin case out of the machine.

Placing a Bobbin Into a Fixed Bobbin Case

Variations in this type of bobbin case are common; consult your machine's manual. A common type works like this:

- Leave approximately 7–8cm of thread hanging from the bobbin. The bobbin is oriented so the thread is counterclockwise, with the tail hanging down, forming the letter P.

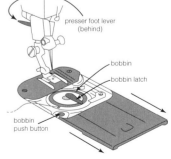

presser foot lever (behind)

bobbin

bobbin latch

bobbin push button

- Place the bobbin on to the centre stud in the bobbin case. Pull the thread to the right and then back to the left. The thread should enter a tension slot. To remove the bobbin, press the bobbin button to release.

Drawing Up the Bobbin Thread

1 Hold the end of the needle thread with the left hand and turn the hand wheel forward with the right hand until the needle is completely lowered into the bobbin area.

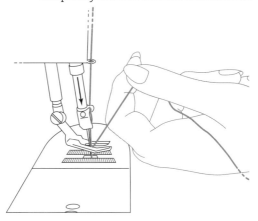

2 Continue to rotate the hand wheel until the needle starts to bring up the bobbin thread. Pull the needle thread toward the front. The bobbin thread loop automatically follows.

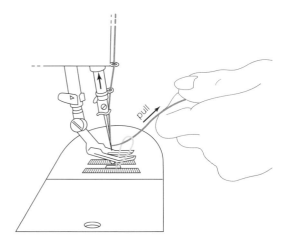

3 Pull the looped bobbin thread towards the front until approximately 7–8cm of thread is visible.

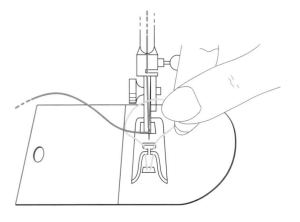

4 Position the needle and bobbin thread under the presser foot, placing them behind the foot.

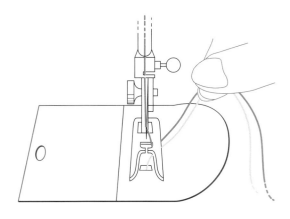

AUTOMATIC THREADER:
Some machines perform all or part of this function automatically.

Stitching Guidelines and Problem Solving

It is not true that sewing machines were designed to confuse the user. However, sewing on a machine that is not working properly can be a frustrating experience. Operating a sewing machine is simple when you understand how to use it properly; be patient and learn to master your machine. Some common problems and their solutions are outlined in the following table.

TABLE 1.6 Common Problems and Solutions

PROBLEM	CHECKLIST
Thread looping on the bottom layer of fabric.	Is the sewing machine threaded correctly? Is the thread in the tension disks properly? (Did you thread with the presser foot up or down?)
Skipped or uneven stitches.	Is the machine needle backwards? Is the machine needle the correct size? Is the sewing machine threaded correctly?
Needle unthreading or breaking.	Is the thread in the tension disks correctly? Is the tension too tight? Is the thread caught on something in the thread path, such as the thread spool? Is the needle blunt? If so, replace it.
Fabric being pulled down into needle hole.	Is the correct throat plate in place? Make sure you use the straight stitch throat plate with a small hole, not the zigzag plate with a wide hole, for straight stitching.
Puckered seams.	Is the machine threaded correctly? If so, check the tension. Use a lower tension setting. Stitch length may require adjustment.
Incorrect upper tension.	Too loose: Stitches appear loose on the top side of the fabric, and links are visible on the underside. Too tight: Stitches pull together on the top side of the fabric and create a pinched effect. Consult your machine's manual to adjust the tensions correctly. For most home sewing machines, an upper tension of about four should work for most fabrics.
Incorrect bobbin tension.	Too loose: Links are visible on the top side of the fabric. Too tight: Stitches appear pinched on the underside of the fabric.

STUDIO TIPS

- If the stitching thread looks incorrect on the bottom layer of fabric, this usually means something is wrong with the upper threading, the tension, or the needle.
- If the stitching thread looks incorrect on the top layer of fabric, this usually means that something is wrong with the bobbin or the threading of the bobbin.
- Many beginners experience the machine thread coming out of the needle because they have not left at least 12–13cm of thread under and behind the presser foot before starting the seam. Also, when starting to sew, the take-up lever should be in its highest position.
- Be sure to clean the machine often to prevent dust buildup and to remove trapped thread or fabric pieces. Follow your machine's instructions for cleaning and oiling with sewing machine oil only.

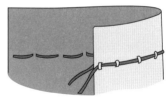

thread looping on bottom layer

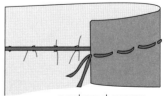

puckered seams

OVERLOCKERS

An overlocker (also known as a serger) supplements but does not replace a sewing machine. The primary purpose of an overlocker is to trim raw edges and overcast the seam edges, creating a clean inside finish and preventing the fabric from ravelling. Industrial machines may be described as overlock machines, overedge machines or merrow machines, a designation going back to the invention of overlock machines by the Merrow Company, patented in 1889.

Unlike traditional sewing machines, overlockers lack bobbins and instead use one or more needle threads and one or more loopers, intertwining the threads for stitch formation. The differential feed function – the ability to have two sets of feed dogs transporting the fabric move at independent rates – enables the overlocker to produce perfectly flat seams in difficult fabrics. Differential feed also allows for some decorative effects, such as shirring or 'lettuce edge' hemming.

Industrial Overlockers

Industrial overlockers tend to be built as single-purpose machines and some are automated. The machine head is set into a table that houses a separate clutch motor, a pedal, a thread stand and an automatic lubrication system. The powerful motor is made to work many hours in a production sewing setting. Industrial overlockers typically make many more stitches per minute than home sewing machines, stitching, overcasting, and trimming seam edges in one step. Seams produced by these machines are narrow and have a professional look. Blindstitch, chain stitch, roll hem and coverstitch functions are also available. Most industrial overlockers bear only faint cosmetic resemblance to their household cousins, but the functions are similar. Brother, Juki, Mauser-Spezial, Pegasus, Pfaff, Singer and Union Special are a few of the brands available. Because overlockers are produced in only a very few factories, and to the specifications of major brands, you might find different branded overlockers that are nearly identical.

Household Overlockers

The market for household overlockers (listed on page 169) has grown in the last 25 years, with models available that can do many decorative stitches as well as construction functions. Household overlockers are usually combination machines, with three- or four-thread overlocking, flatlocking functions, and a rolled (overcast-merrow) hem function as the basic machine. More complex machines offer chain stitching, coverstitching and decorative stitching with multiple needles and threads. The earliest home overlockers were often difficult to thread. Current models of the lightweight machines offer much more convenient threading and can handle several layers of moderately heavy fabrics. A typical stitch rate is around 1,500 stitches per minute, making short work of some tedious tasks like hemming chiffon. Household overlockers are easy to recognize by their multiple tension knobs or dials and cone thread holders. For more information on using an overlocker, please refer to the list of books on page 168.

Purchasing a Household Overlocker

Because of the many functions and features available on overlockers, it is important to comparison shop for price and quality. Consideration should be given to the availability of parts, especially needles. Overlockers commonly do not use the same needles as a home sewing machine. Because overlockers have high stitch rates, it's important to change needles regularly for best sewing results.

Major overlocker types include:

- **A three-thread overlocker** has two loopers and one needle. It is used primarily to overcast seam edges and can also do a three-thread rolled hem stitch and flatlock. Three-thread seams have more stretch than four-thread seaming and are often used for knits.

- **A four-thread overlocker** has two loopers and two needles. It is used to sew and overcast seams at the same time. Most four-thread machines can also produce three-thread stitches. Four-thread overlocking is commonly used for construction seams on woven fabrics.

- **A five-thread overlocker** has three loopers and two needles. This machine is typically used to seam with a two-thread chain stitch as

Overlocker by Babylock

a construction seam while simultaneously overcasting the edge with a three-thread overlock. These machines can usually do a two-thread rolled hem and often can do a two-needle coverstitch.

Many different models of overlockers are available. The least expensive models available in the home market generally will sew three- or four-thread overedge stitching, three-thread rolled hems, and can be used to seam garments. Machines designated as two-five-thread machines will generally do two- and three-thread rolled hems, three- and four-thread overlocking and five-thread safety stitching. Some models will also do coverstitching and chain stitching. Top-of-the-line machines may have ten cones of thread, multiple decorative stitches and amenities like forced air threading of thread paths.

SEWING EQUIPMENT *and* TOOLS

Measuring Tools and Speciality Rulers

The following are the most common sewing tools for measuring:

- **Tape measure** – A flexible 150cm reversible tape used to take various measurements.
- **Crotch tape measure** – A flexible 150cm tape with an attached cardboard piece on one end, used to measure inseams.
- **Yard stick or metre stick** – A 1m wooden or metal ruler used to measure hems, grainlines, flat surfaces and lengths.
- **46cm clear plastic ruler** – A 5cm-wide ruler divided into 3mm grids. A clear ruler is perfect for measuring grainlines and adjusting the pattern at the alteration line. Both metric and imperial rulers are available at office supply stores, fabric stores or online, such as <www.morplan.com>.

- **Sewing gauge** – A 15cm gauge with a movable indicator used to measure areas that need a constant measurement, such as hem widths, pleats and tucks. Many have dual metric and imperial scales.
- **Buttonhole gauge** – An expandable measuring device for spacing buttons and buttonholes quickly and automatically. Available through companies that supply home sewing notions and some fabric stores.
- **Clear plastic fashion ruler** – A see-through plastic ruler with curved lines that enable you to adjust curves. It functions as a combination French curve and hip curve as well as a straight ruler.
- **Hem marker** – A device used to measure the distance from the floor to the bottom of a garment.
- **French curve ruler** – About 25cm long with an edge shaped like a spiral curve. This is used as a guide to shape and true the edges of necklines, armholes, sleeve caps, darts, crotch seams, lapels, pockets and collars.

STUDIO TIP It's good to periodically check your rulers and measuring tapes against one another for consistency. Older measuring tapes in particular tend to stretch out with use.

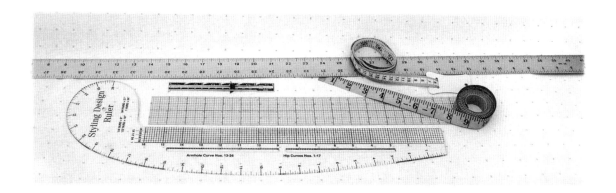

Cutting Tools

The following are some common cutting tools:

- **Scissors and shears** – Blades of shears are usually 10–20cm long and made of steel; one handle on a pair of shears is larger than the other. Bent-handled shears are excellent for easy and correct cutting of fabrics and patterns. Scissors are usually smaller than shears, approximately 7–15cm, and the handles are the same size. For cutting fabric, choose the longest blades you can comfortably cut with.
- **Buttonhole scissors** – Small scissors with sharp points especially designed to cut buttonholes.
- **Pinking shears** – Shears that cut a zigzag edge to prevent fabric from fraying and also create a decorative edge on seam allowances. These shears are not to be used when cutting the first pattern and fabric layout.
- **Seam ripper** – A small, pointed device with a sharp blade. The point can be used to pick out unwanted stitches; the blade is used to cut a row of stitches.
- **Thread nippers** – A specially designed nipper that is useful for cutting stray threads and clipping small areas. Often used for trimming thread tails at the beginning and end of seams.
- **Trimming scissors** – Scissors that are usually 10–20cm long with sharp points and used for clipping threads and trimming or clipping seams.
- **Rotary cutters** – A round blade, cutting device used to cut straight seams with a ruler guiding the blade. Not recommended for cutting curves, because they are not accurate.

STUDIO TIPS

- Scissors and shears require periodic professional sharpening to retain their best cutting quality. Some manufacturers offer a lifetime sharpening and repair service for scissors and shears, with a nominal charge for shipping.
- Sometimes scissors and shears can start feeling 'unsharp', especially after cutting some adhesive-coated materials, certain synthetics or paper. Wipe the blades with a soft cloth moistened with rubbing alcohol to remove residue. Apply a tiny drop of sewing machine oil at the pivot point of the blades.

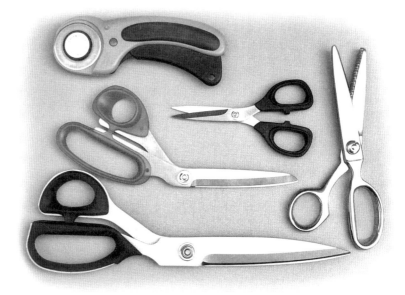

Sewing Tools and Miscellaneous Supplies

The following are useful sewing tools and supplies:

- **Straight pins** – Silk or dressmaker pins made from stainless steel or brass, with sharp tapering points, which do not rust and are safe for use on all fabrics. Ballpoint pins are also used for knit fabrics.
- **Hand sewing needles** – Long, thin steel shafts with an eye at one end. Needles are available in a variety of sizes and types. A packet of assorted needles is recommended.

  - **Sharps needles** – These needles are available in sizes five to ten; they are all-purpose needles and can be used on sheer, fine, lightweight to heavyweight fabrics.
  - **Between needles** – Shorter than sharps, these needles have a small round eye and are meant for short, accurate hand stitches for tailoring and other handwork.
  - **Crewel or embroidery needles** – These needles have a large oval eye and can accommodate heavy or multiple strands of thread. They are the same length as sharps.

- **Thimble** – A lightweight metal (brass, rubber or nickel) device with a closed top that snugly fits the middle finger of the sewing hand. It protects the finger as it pushes the needle through the fabric while hand sewing.
- **Pincushion or pin dispenser** – Keeps pins organized in a convenient place. The most common pincushion is in the shape of a tomato and has a small bag of emery for removing snags or rust from needles or pins. Other types and sizes are available. Select a size and style that you find easiest to use.
- **Beeswax** – Wax, usually in a holder with grooves. Pass the thread through the beeswax to strengthen the thread and reduce its tendency to tangle. Be careful when using beeswax on thread that will be used on fabrics that will be dry-cleaned: the wax will melt into the fabric and might be visible on the fabric surface.
- **Emery cushion** – A small bag filled with abrasive that is used to remove rust and snags from needles or pins.

- **Chalk pencils** – Pencils available in pastel colours that are used to transfer markings from the pattern to the fabric. Markings are made on the wrong side of the fabric and do not show on the correct side; they are washable or evaporate with exposure to air.
- **Tailor's chalk** – Washable clay chalk in thin shapes used to mark fabric at hemlines and other construction lines. Chalk is also available in powdered form in a Chaco Liner or similar dispenser with a small wheel. White chalk will wash out; some fabrics are permanently stained by the coloured chalks. A waxy tailor's chalk is commonly used in the fashion industry.
- **Tracing paper** – A washable, inked, double-coated paper. Position the paper between the wrong sides of two layers of fabric and use a tracing wheel to transfer pattern markings to the fabric. I do not recommend that you use tracing paper, because markings can show through on the correct side of the fabric at times and might not wash out well.
- **Tracing wheel** – A serrated-edge or needle-pointed circular wheel with a handle. Used with or without tracing paper to transfer markings. The wheel portion must be sharp enough to leave an impression, but smooth so it won't snag the fabric.
- **Loop turner** – A device used to turn bias tubing or belts.
- **Safety pins** – Pins used for stringing cording or elastic through casings, or for turning wider tubing.

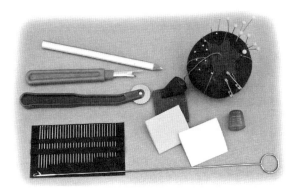

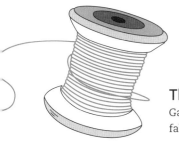

Thread

Garments should be sewn with thread that exactly matches in colour. Thread choice depends on the fabric, the size of the stitch, and the effect desired.

Several types of thread are available for both machine and hand sewing. With all types of thread, the higher the number on the spool, the finer the thread. If the thread is too thick for the fabric, you might see rippling along seam lines as a result of 'thread jamming'.

The following are some of the most common kinds of thread:

- **Corespun thread** – Cotton-wrapped polyester or polyester-wrapped polyester. Suitable for most fabric, this thread has greater strength than spun polyester of the same diameter. This is a matte finished thread that melds into a seam well. Cotton-wrapped polyester can tolerate the high temperatures required for pressing cotton and linen fabric. Lightweight corespun threads are often not available in home sewing supplies but are available for industrial sewing.
- **Spun polyester thread** – A strong thread made of short lengths of polyester fibres spun together. This thread has some give to it and should be used for stretch fabrics and wool fabrics.

- **Mercerized cotton thread** – A cotton thread with a slight sheen, usually available in several thicknesses: 12 weight for topstitching, 30 and 40 weight for general machine sewing or quilting, and 50 and 60 weight for fine fabrics and hand sewing. Use this thread for stitching cotton and linen fabrics.
- **Buttonhole twist** – A thicker thread, size 12, made of cotton, polyester or silk and used for topstitching, hand stitching buttonholes and sewing on buttons.
- **Machine quilting thread** – A lustrous, strong thread made of pure cotton or cotton-wrapped polyester. This is ideal for most hand sewing, because it does not tangle.
- **Overlocker thread** – A spun polyester, lighter than general sewing machine thread, usually on a cone. Overlocker thread can be quite linty or have thick spots and is not recommended for sewing machines..

STUDIO TIP

High-quality threads have longer staples that are best for ensuring good machine performance. Thread with shorter staples or waxed thread will obstruct the machine, reducing the sewing quality.

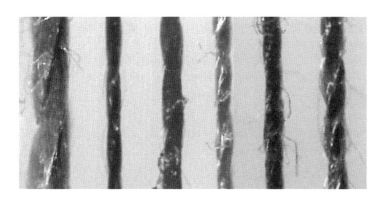

Sewing Machine Needles

Sewing machine needle size should coordinate with the type and weight of fabric and the thread size. The needle should be the smallest size that will produce a good seam in the fabric. If the needle skips, go up a needle size.

Sewing machine needles are specified by needle system, by size and by point style. Domestic sewing machines have used the same needle system for about 40 years, labelled either 130/705H or 15X1H. Industrial sewing machines and overlockers use a variety of needle systems with designators like DBX1 or 85X1. The first number refers to the European system, the second to the American. The higher the number, the thicker the needle.

As the numbers increase in both systems, the shank of the needle gets larger in diameter, as does the eye of the needle and the long groove at the front of the needle. Needles are available in sizes 8/60 to 18/110 for home machines and in a broader range for industrial machines. Size 8/60 or 9/65 are used for sewing fine or sheer fabrics; most medium-weight fabrics are sewn with sizes ranging from 10/70 to 12/80 needles; and heavier weight fabrics are sewn with the 14/90 or 16/100 sizes.

The drawings illustrate typical sewing machine needles that are produced by a number of needle manufacturers. Check the packaging when purchasing sewing machine needles; it should list the machine style, needle size and the point style.

The following are some of the most common types of sewing machine needles:

- **Universal point needle** – The most common needle type, suitable for most woven fabric. It is available in a variety of needle sizes from 8/60 (for lightweight fabrics) to 18/110 (for heavyweight fabrics). Variations of the universal needle point include such styles as Microtex, for silks and closely woven fabrics, including microfibres.
- **Ballpoint needle** – The rounded point on this needle makes it ideal for use on all types of knits or stretch fabrics. It is available in the same sizes as universal. Variations include stretch points for elastic and stretch fabrics.

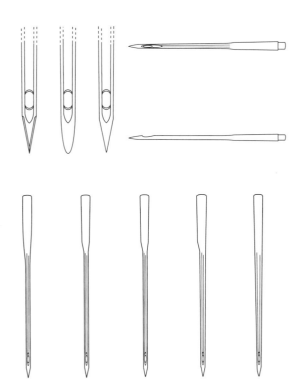

- **Wedge-shaped needle, also called a leather needle** – A special needle used for leather, suede and some artificial leathers and vinyl. Available in sizes 10/70 to 19/120. This needle is not for use on most fabrics.

METRIC-EQUIVALENT NEEDLE SIZES:
NM, the metric size of a needle, gives the diameter of the needle blade in hundredths of a millimetre, so the blade of a size NM100 needle is 1mm in diameter.

INDUSTRIAL SHANK VS DOMESTIC SHANK NEEDLES:
Round shank needles are used for industrial machines whereas flat shank needles are used for domestic machines. The flat shank needle allows for easy replacement and ensures that the needle is in the correct position.

MATCHING THREAD AND NEEDLE SIZES

Thread that is too thick for the eye of the needle can cause loops to form on the underside of the fabric being sewn. Threads should be about half the diameter of the needle eye. A quick test to see if needle and thread size are a good match is to cut a length of sewing thread about 30cm long and thread it through the eye of a loose machine needle. Hold the thread taut between your hands and spin the needle around the thread while dropping one hand so the thread is at a 45-degree angle. If the needle slips down the thread as you quit spinning it, the eye is large enough for the thread size chosen.

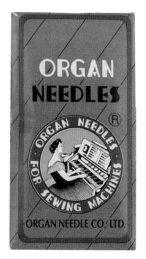

STUDIO TIP

Replace needles if they are dull, bent or blunt – commonly the result of hitting a pin or presser foot but also by wear as the needle penetrates the fabrics. Dull or bent needles will cause skipped stitches and can damage fabric. It is a good idea to have extra sewing machine needles on hand.

TABLE 1.7 Fabric and Needle Size

TYPE OF FABRIC	FABRIC WEIGHT	NEEDLE SIZE	NEEDLE TYPE
Woven fabrics	Light	8/60, 9/65	Universal
	Medium	10/70, 11/75, 12/80	Universal
	Heavy	14/90, 16/100, 110/18	Universal or jeans needle
Pile and nap woven		11/75, 12/80, 14/90	Universal
Knit and stretch fabrics	Light	8/60, 9/65	Ballpoint or stretch
	Medium	10/70, 11/75, 12/80	Ballpoint or stretch
	Heavy	14/90, 16/100	Ballpoint or stretch
Pile and nap knit		11/75, 12/80, 14/90	Ballpoint or stretch
Leather, leather-type suede, and vinyl fabrics	Heavy	18/110, 19/120	Leather or wedge

PRESSING EQUIPMENT *and* TOOLS

Pressing is essential to complete a professional-looking garment. Using the pressing tools will ensure that all areas are correctly pressed to improve the overall look of the garment. The following are helpful pieces of pressing equipment:

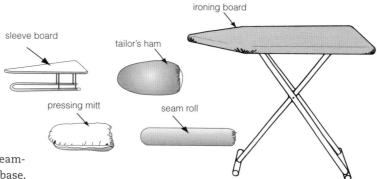

- **Ironing board** – A sturdy surface with a narrow end, it is adjustable to various heights.
- **Iron (steam and dry)** – A steam-and-dry iron with a wide range of temperature controls is the most effective tool for pressing the many varieties of fashion fabrics. A steam-generated iron, with a separate base, is the best type of iron to give a finished professional press.
- **Needle board** – A small, rectangular board covered with wire needles. This board is used when pressing napped or pile fabrics such as velvet and corduroy. The needles prevent the pile from matting or crushing. A common needle board substitute is a special pile fabric.
- **Pounding block** – A smooth, hardwood block used on fabric while it is still moist from steam, for making strong creases on trousers, collars, hems, pleats and facings.
- **Pressing cloth** – A piece of cotton or muslin. The pressing cloth is usually dampened, folded and placed between the fabric and the iron. While applying some pressure and heat from the iron, the pressing cloth will protect the correct side of the garment from shine and results in a clean press.
- **Pressing mitt** – A small, padded mitten used to press and maintain contoured seams such as sleeve caps and areas that should not be pressed flat.

- **Seam roll** – A small cylindrical, long, firmly padded cushion, covered with a woven cotton on one side and wool on the other. This is used to press long, narrow seams in hard-to-reach areas such as sleeve seams. The cotton side is used to press most fabrics, and the wool side to press woollens.
- **Sleeve board** – A small, padded ironing board with ends that are different sizes. This board sits on top of a regular ironing board and is used to press sleeves and other small areas.
- **Tailor's board** – A wooden tool that tapers to a narrow point, used to press difficult-to-reach areas such as collars, lapels and points or corners.
- **Tailor's ham** – An ovoid, lightweight cushion that is firmly padded and covered with heavy cotton on one side and wool on the other. Used to press contoured seams, darts, collars and lapels. The cotton side is used to press most fabrics, and the wool side to press woollens.

PRESSING METHODS

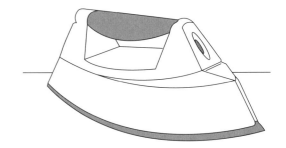

Using the correct iron temperature, some pressure and appropriate pressing tools will ensure that all areas are correctly pressed for a professionally finished garment.

Iron temperature control – Most irons have a temperature range from cool to hot. If an iron is too hot, it could distort, melt, scorch or leave an impression on the fabric. If it is too cool, it may not press the fabric. Test the iron temperature with a small swatch of the fabric selected for the garment.

The following are the steps for pressing seams and darts:

1 Press all seams flat, to one side. This allows the stitches to settle into the fabric. Then press the seam open.

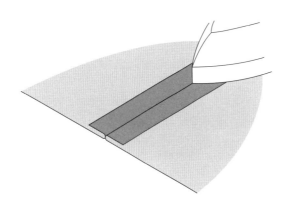

2 Press the excess of darts toward the centre of the garment or down. A tailor's ham helps to build in the shape created by the dart.

3 Press all seams and darts from the wrong side of the fabric.

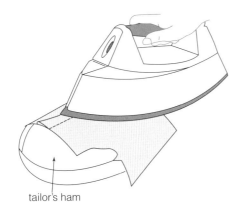

tailor's ham

STUDIO TIPS

- Spitting steam irons – A steam iron set to a cool temperature can cause the iron to 'spit' or drizzle water, often discolouring the fabric. If you will be pressing fabric requiring a temperature below the steam mark on your iron, try pressing scrap fabric for 30 seconds to make sure the iron doesn't spit. If it does spit, you might wish to use a damp press cloth and a dry iron for pressing.
- When pressing, place a strip of paper between the dart and the fabric to prevent an impression of the dart appearing on the correct side of the garment. Paper can also be used under ordinary seam allowances when pressing.

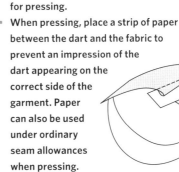

paper

To ensure a professional-looking finished garment, the following are important pressing techniques:

- Lift and lower the iron. Do not pull the iron back and forth across the fabric. Pressing is done to shape and flatten seams. Ironing, a side-to-side motion, is used for removing wrinkles.
- Press each area of the garment as it is sewn, before continuing to another sewing step.
- If a flatter, cleaner pressing job is desired, lightly dampen a pressing cloth. Place the damp pressing cloth between the iron and the garment to create more steam. Continue to use the steam setting on the iron and apply a bit more pressure.

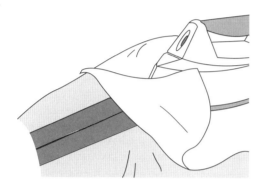

- When pressing any napped or pile fabric such as velvet and corduroy, be sure to lay the correct side of the fabric over a needle board and press from the wrong side of the garment.

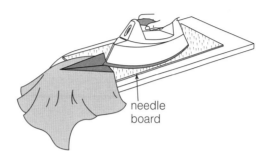

needle board

- Use a small seam roll to press long, narrow seams. Use a sleeve board for small areas.

seam roll

STUDIO TIP

If a sleeve board is unavailable, use a towel or piece of cotton fabric and roll it very tightly into a cylinder shape. Tie the two ends of the cylinder with ribbon or yarn and insert into the sleeve, then press.

CHAPTER

2

IDENTIFYING FASHION FABRICS

- An Introduction to Fabrics
- Organic and Natural Fabrics
- Neither Natural nor Synthetic
- Synthetic and Man-made Fibres
- Linings
- Interfacings

AN INTRODUCTION TO FABRICS

The newest fabrics have been inspired by mounting global environmental awareness, the effects of pollution and the desire to produce quality fabric with less impact upon the environment. New natural fibres and noble mixtures spin a perfect fabric story, with effects ranging from the most refined to the rustic.

Fabric Texture

The biggest news in fabrics today is that mills are combining organic fibres with high-tech machines. This was brought about by the continuing search for fabrics with the desirable characteristics of 'newness'. At first glance, the newest fabrics and threads might appear classic, but innovative complexities in the finish of the fabric, including lacquered, metallized, gauzed, washed-out, wrinkled and twisted, have resulted in fabrics that are lighter, more durable and possess a finer hand.

The quality of the raw materials and the use of subtle variations are combined to give new looks to the surface, appearance and hand of fabric. For instance, blends dubbed 'techno-natural' are mostly a mix of natural fibres with synthetics, creating some remarkable effects. Mills are also blending natural fibres with cashmere, silk and wool to give fabrics a look of lightness, fluffiness and warmth. Fine fabrics, such as cashmere, baby alpaca, kid mohair and extra-fine woollens, have acquired a classy yet simple finish that is felted, matted, scrubbed, hairy or primitive. Wool, hemp and silk are combined with polyester to obtain subtle differences in appearance and hand, whereas raffia and paper are combined with cotton or linen to create a more textured effect.

New processing techniques for cottons create lustrous and soft glossy fabric. In addition, natural fibres are blended with synthetics and other natural fibres. For example, wool and cotton blends and wool and linen blends have been accepted in the marketplace. New fabrics include micro textures created with micro weaves, resulting in fabrics with lightness, highgrade performance and a dreamlike hand.

The process of producing fabric is the same, regardless of the fabric's texture or the type of fibre. Fibres are twisted together to form yarns. The yarns are then woven or knitted to form a fabric. Colour is applied either by dyeing or printing. Finally, a finishing technique (usually chemical) is applied to improve the performance and provide fabric characteristics desirable to the customer and suitable for end use.

Fibres

The choice of fibres and the production methods with which these fibres are put together, define the differences among fabrics. Fibres are either natural or manufactured. Natural fibres from plants include: cotton linen/flax, hemp, ramie, maize and jute. Animal fibres include: sheep/wool, angora goat (mohair), angora rabbit (angora), camel and alpaca. Buffalo down fibre is gaining popularity in commercial and hand knitting. Silk is the only fibre obtained from an insect (silkworm).

Manufactured fibres are not found in nature and are produced using a variety of chemical processes. Manufactured fibres include: acetate, acrylic, nylon, polyester, rayon, spandex and Tencel. Plant matter, such as wood, bamboo, seaweed and soy, is crushed to a pulp and then broken down further with the use of a chemical solution. The solutions are then forced through tiny holes of a spinneret (similar to water passing through a shower head) to transform them into continuous strands called filament fibres.

Microfibre fabrics are very soft and drape well. In addition, microfibre technology creates fabric that looks and feels like silk. It is also possible to produce thin, lightweight linen and washable, non-felting woollens, both with a silk-like hand. The most common types of microfibres are made from polyesters, polyamides (nylon), or a conjugation of polyester and polyamide. Metallic fibres are made into thin strip yarns from gold, silver, copper, stainless steel and aluminum. These yarns are woven into fabric by wrapping around a core of another fibre. Fabric can also be made by using 100 per cent of one fibre or by combining different fibres. Blends are usually created when a fibre does not possess adequate properties desired for the intended purpose. For example, cotton wrinkles easily while possessing desirable qualities of absorbency and softness. Blending cotton with polyester, which has excellent wrinkle resistance, produces a wrinkle-resistant, absorbent, soft fabric.

Eco-friendly Fibres

The eco-sustainability issue is generating significant change in the fashion industry. New developments in harvesting and processing of animal and vegetable fibres are resulting in eco-fibres, finer denier wools and thinner and softer yarns. A class of functional, eco-sustainable fibres is being created from advances in technology, altered dyeing techniques and the use of salvaged clothing, organic cotton, recycled plastics and other materials.

The demand for fibres created from organic cultivation methods and recycled and biodegradable materials, has resulted in the use of organic cotton, hemp, linen, ramie, bamboo, soy, maize and cellulose. In addition to the demand for eco-friendly fibre and fabrics, the industry is also developing dyes and finishing processes that conserve energy. Wool is a renewable resource, because the fibre is shorn from the animal. The animal's life is maintained for wool production for many years.

These new fabrics, as well as traditional textiles, offer unlimited arrays of weaves, patterns and colours. Through the use of technology, these new fibres are being blended with traditional, synthetic and man-made fibres in unlimited combinations.

In addition to garments, the fashion eco-sustainability movement includes clothing labels and buttons. Labels are increasingly produced from leather, wool, paper and organic cotton. The use of real horn, vegetable ivory and mother-of-pearl as base material for buttons is accelerating.

Blended Fabrics

Fabric blends comprise two or more different types of fibres twisted or spun together. By blending fibres, the qualities of the fabric are enhanced.

Designed for easy care, most blended fabrics possess greater durability, softer or more luxurious hand, increased wrinkle resistance and reduction or elimination of shrinkage than the original fibre. The type and amount of fibres used in a blend are identified on the bolt.

Thanks to today's technology, the type and number of blends is almost unlimited. Any fibre can be combined with any other fibre. The selection of fibres determines the properties and characteristics of the resulting fabric. The addition of Lycra to many woven and knit fabrics is now common. As the production and processing of natural, synthetic and man-made fibres is changing rapidly, fabrics will continue to evolve.

Testing Fibre Content

There are regulations in place around the world that require uncut fabrics to be labelled and identified with the correct fibre content and care instructions. It is important to know fibre content for correct fabric handling. For example, the fabric might require preshrinking before cutting. This information is usually noted on the end of the fabric bolt. If the information is missing or incomplete, the salesperson may be of assistance.

If the fibre content of a fabric is unknown a simple burn test, with analysis of the ash and other burn characteristics, can be used to determine fibre content. To conduct a burn test, hold a small swatch of fabric with a pair of tweezers over a non-flammable surface. Touch the fabric with a lighted match. Place the swatch directly into the flame and observe how it burns. Does the piece burn slowly or self-extinguish? Does it burn quickly, melt or drip? Then, allow the sample to cool and check the colour and texture of the ash. Does the ash resemble the fabric weave or a melted hard bead?

Note the following fibres:

- **Cotton** and **rayon** burn quickly and smell like burning paper with white smoke. They leave behind a feathery grey ash that floats away.
- **Linen** ignites slowly and leaves a light, feathery grey ash in the shape of the fabric weave. It smells like burning leaves.
- **Wool** burns slowly and has a distinctive 'hair' odour. Wool ash is easily crushed, feels crispy and leaves a sooty residue.
- **Silk** burns similarly to wool with an unpleasant odour. The ash is a more delicate, puffy black ash.
- **Bamboo** burns quickly with a soft, dark brownish ash. It smells like burning leaves.
- **Synthetics** burn with a hot flame, melt and drip. When the ash cools, it can be crushed between the fingers but leaves an oily residue. Synthetic fibres leave a black bead, a hard bead, or a sticky mass.
- **Acetate** burns quickly with a hot vinegar odour. It leaves a hard, irregular-shaped black bead.

Grainlines

It is important to understand the basic details of fabric structure. Grains indicate yarn direction. The *lengthwise grain* is also known as the *warp*, the *crosswise grain* is the *weft*. Intersecting the grain and crossgrain is known as the *bias* direction. Each grain has different characteristics that influence the manner in which the fabric will drape on the body.

Lengthwise grain (straight of grain)

The lengthwise grain of the fabric is always parallel to the *selvedge* of the fabric and is also referred to as the warp. The *selvedge* is the firmly woven edge that runs the length of the fabric on both sides, also known as lengthwise grain. The strongest threads (*warp*) run in the lengthwise direction and possess less give (stretch) than the crossgrain. The lengthwise grain is placed vertically in the garment in most designs.

Crosswise grain

The crosswise grain, or *crossgrain*, is the section of the weave that runs perpendicular to the lengthwise grain of the fabric from selvedge to selvedge. These crossgrain yarns are the *filling yarns* or *weft*. The crossgrain of woven fabric has slightly more give (stretch) than the lengthwise grain. The crosswise grain is placed horizontally in the garment, which gives a fuller look to the garment.

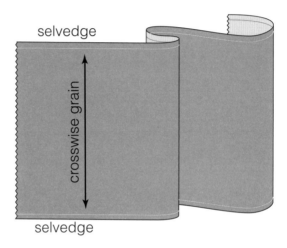

Bias

The bias direction possesses significantly more give and stretch than either lengthwise or crosswise grain. Bias-cut garments create draped contours that fall gracefully over the body. To find the bias, fold the lengthwise grain of the fabric to the crossgrain to create a perfect 45-degree fold line. The resulting 45-degree line is called *true bias*.

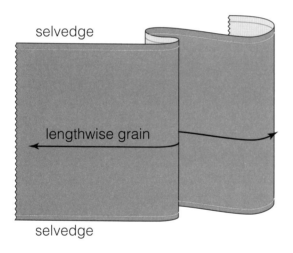

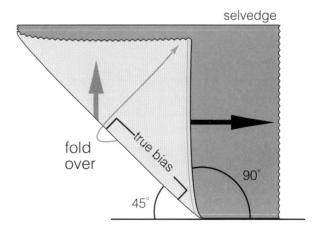

Fabric Construction

There are several methods to create fabric from yarns, fibres and filaments. The two most common methods of creating fabrics are weaving and knitting.

WOVEN FABRIC

Woven fabric comprises two sets of yarns – warp and weft. The warp is the lengthwise yarn. The weft is the filling or crosswise yarn. The warp and weft yarns cross at right angles. Yarns can be interlaced to form a **plain weave**, **twill weave** or **satin weave**. Other weaves include basket, jacquard and pile.

A common characteristic of all woven fabric is that it frays at the cut edge – the looser the weave, the more the cut edge frays. Fabric durability usually increases as the tightness or density of the weave increases.

COMMON WOVEN FABRICS

Examples of common woven fabrics include: batiste, broadcloth, calico, chambray, corduroy, denim, flannel, gabardine, gauze, georgette, gingham, linen, muslin, organza, poplin, seersucker, silk, sharkskin, taffeta, tweed, velvet, velveteen and voile.

STUDIO TIP

A finished seam edge on woven fabric ensures durability and easy care. This can be accomplished by overlocking the seam edges.

PLAIN WEAVE

Each weft yarn passes over and under each of the warp yarns going in the opposite direction.

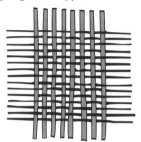

TWILL WEAVE

Twill weave has diagonal lines in the fabric. Yarns cross at least two yarns before going under one or more yarns.

SATIN WEAVE

Yarn goes over one and under several to create more lustre on the correct side of the fabric.

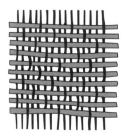

KNITS

An important characteristic of a knitted fabric is its capacity to stretch. A knitted fabric is constructed by interlocking looped yarns and any fibre can be knitted into fabric. Knit fabrics vary in appearance by fibre content as well as type of knit. Knit fabrics possess the characteristics of the fibres used to make the knit. Knits are available in a variety of fibres, weights, textures and patterns. Used in a wide variety of garments, the knit selected must be appropriate for the design.

SINGLE KNIT

One set of needles is used to form loops across the fabric width. Single and jersey knits are light- to medium-weight fabrics. Unlike double knits, single and jersey knits stretch approximately 20 per cent across the grain. These knits have flat vertical ribs on the right side of the fabric, and horizontal lines dominate the wrong side. Single knit is commonly used for T-shirts.

DOUBLE KNIT

Two sets of needles are used to make double knits, giving both sides of the fabric a similar appearance. Double knits are medium- to heavyweight, with both sides of the fabric appearing the same. These fabrics possess good body and shape retention.

TRICOT KNIT

Several loops formed in a lengthwise direction. Tricot, a single knit, usually made with very fine yarn, is used primarily for lingerie and lightweight linings. The right side of these knits has vertical ribs and crosswise stretch.

COMMON KNIT FABRICS

Common knit fabrics, depending on the fibre, weave and weight, are sweatshirt fleece, velour, stretch velvet, sweater knit, textured novelty knits, two-way stretch spandex, ribbing and fleece. These knits might be made of acrylic, polyester, cotton, wool or blends and are available in a wide variety of weights. Some, such as fleece, may be made of recycled plastic material.

STUDIO
TIPS

- Variations in the pattern of knits are achieved by changing the arrangement of the basic stitch or loop.
- Single and jersey knits, double knits and rib knits, known as weft knits, display a characteristic vertical line and stretch more in width than length.
- Novelty and tricot knits, known as warp knits, possess less stretch and more resistance to runs than weft knits.

ORGANIC *and* NATURAL FABRICS

Organic fabrics – The following conditions apply to the production of organic fabrics: no use of pesticides, no use of chemical additives, no use of substances harmful to the health of humans or animals and no use of invasive techniques for looking after animals.

Natural fabrics – These fabrics are produced from natural fibres but do not have to be manufactured under the organic standards stated above. Fabrics made from natural fibres include cotton from the cotton plant, linen that is processed from the flax plant, wool from sheep and silk from silkworms. Until the early twentieth century, these fabrics were the standard bearers for making garments.

Technological advances – Technological advancements have modernized the natural fabrics (cotton, linen, silk and wool). Careful research and mill creativity, manufacturing processes, and the use of microfibres, dyes and blending of fibres are making it possible to imitate all the natural fibres as never before. In addition to the standard four natural fibres, new basic fibres – including hemp, bamboo and ramie – have been developed for use in fabrics. It is now possible to alter base fibres, old and new, blend with other fibres, texturize and enhance the finish. Individually and/or collectively applied, these advancements give these fabrics new properties and characteristics suitable for today's designs. The newest combinations are referred to as 'Techno-Natural', such as wool and silk with polyester.

COTTON

Cotton is a very versatile natural fabric. The properties of cotton – affordability, easy care, strength, durability and comfort – have made it the world's principal clothing fabric.

A long growing season is essential for successful cotton cultivation. The cotton plant begins to grow after the blossom falls off. When bolls open and white fibres are visible, the cotton is harvested. The boll's fibres are used in fabric production, with the seeds removed and used to produce oils and other by-products.

There are two primary differences between traditionally produced cotton and organic cotton: organic cotton must comply with organic producers' standards and the finishing processes used in fabric production. Owing to these differences, organic cotton is expensive compared with traditionally produced cotton. This price disparity could change as large clothing companies continue to blend organic cotton with other fibres.

COTTON CATEGORIES

Lightweight – Batiste, chiffon, gauze, lawn, organdie, voile. These fabrics can be used for dress or eveningwear, layered fashion and for linings, underlinings and stabilizers.

Medium weight – Bouclé, chambray, chintz (polished cotton), damask, denim, flannel, gabardine, gingham, muslin, shirting, pique, plisse, poplin, seersucker, twill and velveteen. These fabrics can be used for sportswear, casual clothing, men's shirts, children's clothes, sleepwear, blouses and dresses.

Heavyweight – Bouclé, brocade, chenille, corduroy, damask, denim, duck, gabardine, matelassé, terrycloth, twill, velour, velvet and velveteen. These are used for eveningwear, sportswear, dresses, jackets, sleepwear, tailored garments and children's wear.

LINEN

Linen, made from the flax plant, has been in use for more than 4,000 years. Flax is grown in many parts of the world, making it one of the most easily accessible materials for textile production.

Linen fabric possesses a characteristic uneven weave. Linen feels cool and dry to the touch because it can absorb up to 20 times its weight in moisture before becoming damp. The fibres possess a hollow core that keeps moisture away from the body, helping to inhibit mould and fungus growth and giving it antibacterial properties.
The finished fabric might appear rougher than cotton or it might appear smooth with even weaves, as in fine Irish linen, Belgian linen or

handkerchief linen. Although linen is strong and durable (improving with age and laundering), it is also biodegradable, colourfast, moth resistant, non-allergenic and dyes well. Although linen wrinkles easily, it is resistant to wear and abrasion.

LINEN CATEGORIES
Lightweight – Gauze and handkerchief. Suitable for evening dresses, blouses and skirts.

Medium weight – Suitable for shirts, blouses, dresses and children's clothing.

Heavyweight – Suitable for trousers, tailored dresses, sportswear, jackets, suits and coats.

SILK

For centuries, the most luxurious fabric has been silk. Silk is a versatile fibre, created by the tiny silkworm, which can be manufactured into the lightest of chiffons or ornately brocaded satin or matelassé. As with any natural fibre, different areas of the world produce different types of silk. Although many fabrics dye well, none compare to the intense rich lustre of silk. Silk is also soft, durable, absorbent and delicate in appearance. Although silk resists wrinkles (particularly medium and heavyweight), it is prone to static.

Silkworms are the larvae or caterpillar of the domesticated silk moth, which is native to northern China. In the production of silk, trays of silkworm cocoons are exposed to extreme temperatures so the worm dies before the chrysalis (moth) has a chance to break through the cocoon, preserving the precious silk fibres within the cocoon. A single cocoon produces around 300–600m of silk filament. About 2,000 to 3,000 cocoons are required to make a pound of silk. The quality of filaments reeled together and the methods used in twisting the reeled filaments determine the quality of the finished silk fibre.

Pure silk can be dyed in many colours, resulting in lively prints and finely shaded jacquard weaves. Many lighter and medium silk fabrics can be gently washed and hung to dry; however, dry-cleaning is recommended for heavier silk fabrics and tailored silk garments.

Lightweight – Chiffon, gazar, georgette, mesh, organza, tulle, silk batiste and China silk. Suitable for eveningwear, blouses, skirts and underlinings (especially in heavier silks).

Medium weight – Soft and fluid silks: crêpe de Chine, charmeuse, satin-back crêpe, velvet, knit jersey and jacquard. **Crisp silks**: taffeta, satin and brocade. Soft and fluid silks are suitable for dresses, eveningwear, soft trousers, skirts and jackets. Crisp silks, richer and heavier than other medium-weight silks, are especially suited for bridal gowns, mother of the bride and eveningwear.

Heavyweight/textured silks – Doupioni, shantung, twill, tweeds, and noil (raw silk). These silks have characteristic textured surfaces created from the use of varied silk yarns and weaving techniques. Suitable for tailored garments, trousers, sportswear, and evening wear.

STUDIO TIP

When sewing silk, use very sharp, unblemished needles and sharp cutting tools, otherwise the fabric may snag.

WOOL

The eco-friendly characteristics of animal fibres have been used for clothing for centuries. Wool fabric is obtained from sheep, goats, rabbits and a variety of other animals, including camels and alpaca. Cashmere is obtained from Kashmir goats (India). Alpaca wool comes from the alpaca, a member of the camel family. Angora goats produce mohair yarns and angora rabbits produce angora fibre.

New spinning processes aid in the development of wool sheep fibres, where microns are getting even finer, for a softer touch. Making wool smoother has created a luxurious, silk-like lustre with fluidity, drape and comfort. New air-spinning techniques create airy, incomparably light yarns, reducing their weight to almost half.

Wool animal fibres are warm, soft and durable and are wrinkle and flame resistant. In addition, wool animal fabrics are easy to sew and tailor. They keep moisture away from the body, helping the wearer stay dry. Animal fibre wool absorbs up to 30 per cent of its weight before feeling wet. However, wool weakens and stretches when wet. Wool also felts (mats) when exposed to moisture, heat and pressure.

Lightweight – Broadcloth and challis. Suitable for eveningwear, dresses, scarves, skirts, tops and trousers.

Medium weight – Flannel, gabardine, herringbone twill, houndstooth check, tweed, worsted (broadcloth). Suitable for men's and women's suits and coats, tailored garments, skirts, trousers, sportswear, play clothes and sports coats.

Heavyweight – Loden, tweed and melton. Suitable for coats and other outerwear.

Other Natural Fibres

For centuries, the garment industry's standard bearers of cotton, flax (linen), silk and wool have been joined by the introduction of other natural fibres. Modern technology has enabled the development and introduction of other natural fabrics like ramie, hemp and bamboo. These new fabrics are being mainstreamed into the garment industry. Additionally, these fibres are being blended with many other natural and synthetic fibres, creating unique new fabrics.

RAMIE

Ramie is one of the oldest plant fibres and has been used for thousands of years. The fibres need chemical treatment to remove the gums and pectins found in the bark. Ramie fibres are made into fabric using a process similar to manufacturing linen from flax. Ramie is frequently blended with other fibres to capitalize on its unique strength and absorbency, lustre and dye-affinity. Common fabrics used for blending include cotton, wool, rayon, silk and polyester. The properties of ramie include: resistance to bacteria and mildew; absorbency; resistance to staining; strong when wet; smooth lustrous appearance, which improves with washing; retention of shape; resistance to shrinkage; low abrasion resistance; and durability. Ramie is low in elasticity and wrinkles and is stiffer than linen.

HEMP

Obtained from the hemp plant, hemp fibre is one of the strongest and most durable of all natural textile fibres. In addition, hemp holds its shape and stretches less than any other natural fibre. Known for durability, hemp fabric is comfortable to wear and drapes well. Hemp blends well with a wide variety of natural and synthetic fibres.

Hemp is naturally resistant to mould, accepts dye well, and is very absorbent. The more hemp is used and laundered, the softer it becomes. Hemp is also ultraviolet light (UV) resistant. The porous nature of hemp allows it to 'breathe' so that it feels cool in warm weather. Conversely, hemp clothing traps air (body heat) in the fibres, making hemp garments naturally warm in cooler weather.

REGENERATED FIBRES (NEITHER NATURAL NOR SYNTHETIC)

BAMBOO

Bamboo is a regenerated fibre produced from bamboo pulp. Most fabric made from bamboo uses a chemical manufacturing process used to produce lyocell from wood. This fabric possesses the following characteristics: soft hand; good drape; absorbency; and easy dyeing for quality colour. Like hemp, bamboo fabric is antibacterial and provides some natural UV protection. As a result, bamboo fabric is appropriate for a variety of garments, including swimwear, intimate apparel and garments.

RAYON

Rayon fabric is produced by combining wood pulp and a chemical mixture. Rayon has properties similar to cotton, linen or silk. Rayon is soft, drapeable, durable and dyes well. There are two types of rayon fabric commonly available: *viscose rayon*, which is weak when wet, becoming unstable and shrinking; and *polynosic (Modal) rayon*, which is the strongest variety and is more stable when wet. The use of rayon microfibres produces fabric that has improved drapeability with a silk-like hand and appearance.

Rayon is absorbent, breathable, antistatic, soft and abrasion resistant. It accepts a dye process and wrinkles easily. Rayon is frequently blended with a large variety of other fibres and is used in most categories of ready-to-wear clothing. Although manufacturers might recommend dry-cleaning, rayon can be gently washed either by hand or machine in cold water, using soft hand soap, then line dried.

LYOCELL (TENCEL)

Lyocell, neither man-made nor synthetic, is derived from wood pulp. It is not considered a natural fibre because it is produced using nanotechnology. It is frequently blended with a wide variety of other fibres. Tencel is recognized as the first fibre resulting from nanotechnological developments. Lenzing Textile Fibers in the United States is currently the only major manufacturer of lyocell. The company markets the product under the brand name Tencel.

Tencel is absorbent, breathable, biodegradable, soft and strong, accepts a dye process and is wrinkle resistant. It is also known for its luxurious hand and appearance. Many top designers are producing garments containing Tencel because of the luxurious feel of the fabric. Finished garments should be dry-cleaned or carefully hand washed and line dried. Tencel shrinks by about three per cent when first washed.

SYNTHETIC and MAN-MADE FIBRES

Initially, synthetic, man-made fibres were developed in the search for a substitute for silk. Acetate and rayon were the first synthetic fibres commercially available, followed by nylon, acetate, acrylic, polyester, spandex and Tencel.

Synthetic fabrics gained quick acceptance because they are less expensive than most natural fibres. In general, synthetics are non-absorbent, durable, quick drying, wrinkle resistant, shrink resistant and capable of accepting dye. Synthetic fabrics are available in a variety of textures and forms, including textured, pleated, crinkled, beaded and metallic.

NYLON

Nylon is a generic designation for a family of synthetic polymers known generically as polyamides. An early man-made fibre, nylon was produced commercially in 1939. By 1940, it was knitted into hosiery and was in wide use during World War II for parachutes, flak vests, uniforms and tyres.

Nylon is lightweight, very strong, durable and drapeable. It is prone to static and does not breathe but it dries quickly. Nylon blends well with many other fibres, resulting in increased durability, shape retention and abrasion resistance. It is often blended with velvet and other napped fabrics to help eliminate or reduce crushing. Nylon is used for hosiery, intimate apparel, sportswear, jackets, trousers, skirts, raincoats and children's wear.

ACETATE

Acetate was developed early in the twentieth century. It is cellulose based, made from either cotton or wood pulp. By 1924, an acetate filament yarn was commercially spun by DuPont and trademarked Celanese. Acetate fabric is lustrous with a silk-like look, which drapes well and accepts dye. Because acetate is resistant to shrinkage and moth and mildew damage, it is widely used for linings and evening attire. Acetate is frequently blended with other fibres to reduce pilling.

ACRYLIC

Acrylic was first commercially produced about 1950 from synthetic polymer as an imitation for wool. Acrylic is a fine, soft fabric with good drapability. It dyes well, breathes and absorbs and releases moisture quickly. Comfortable to wear, acrylic is moth resistant, colourfast and is an easy-care fabric. Acrylic is similar in appearance to that of wool, cotton or blended fabric; however, it is susceptible to abrasion, pilling and static electricity. Acetate is frequently used in the manufacture of knitted garments, including sweaters, socks, fleece and sportswear.

POLYESTER

Polyester is made from synthetic polymers and was first commercially produced in 1953. Polyester fabric is highly wrinkle resistant and retains its shape. It is very strong and has a soft hand. It dries quickly and can be heat treated to hold pleats or other shapes permanently. Care is minimal and the fabric is washable. Polyester can assume a variety of forms; for example, it can imitate silk or take the form of fibre fill for pillows and comforters. Polyester blends well with many other fabrics. Blending polyester with other fabrics improves the durability of the fabric, increases wrinkle resistance, eliminates or reduces crushing of napped fabric and reduces fading.

SPANDEX

Spandex is a synthetic fibre that was invented in 1959. It has elastic properties and is capable of stretching up to 600 times and returning to its natural shape. In addition to its comfort and flexibility, it accepts dye well. The presence of spandex in a fabric provides elasticity and stretch. Although commonly used in activewear and swimwear, spandex is increasingly found in daywear, sportswear, children's clothes and eveningwear.

Blended Fabrics

Fabric blends comprise two or more different types of fibres twisted or spun together. By blending fibres, the qualities of the fabric are enhanced. The fibre with the highest percentage of the blend will determine the characteristics and properties of the fabric. For example, a fabric blended of 70 per cent cotton and 30 per cent polyester would have more characteristics of cotton than polyester. Thanks to today's technology, the type and number of blends are almost unlimited. Any fibre can be combined with any other fibre. The selection of fibres determines the properties and characteristics of the resulting fabric.

Designed for easy care, most blended fabrics possess greater durability, softer or more luxurious hand and increased wrinkle resistance than the original fibres, as well as reduction or elimination of shrinkage The type and amount of each fibre used in a blend are identified on the bolt.

The addition of spandex to many woven and knit fabrics is now common. Because the production and processing of natural, synthetic and man-made fibres is changing rapidly, fabrics will continue to evolve.

Fabrics with Pile or Nap

PILE FABRICS

Pile fabrics are three-dimensional, with a surface of upright yarns cut or looped with a knitted or woven backing. Some simulate the look of real fur. Pile fabrics are beautiful, functional, durable and provide added warmth. They can be produced from a variety of fibres and blends. Pile fabrics include bouclé, chenille, corduroy, faux fur, fleece, terrycloth, velour, velveteen and velvet.

NAPPED FABRICS

Napped fabrics have an external covering of fine fibre ends forming the surface and lying smoothly in one direction. The fibre ends might by clipped, brushed or upright. Flannel, fleece, melton, brushed or sueded fabrics, camel hair and all piled fabrics are examples of napped fabrics.

CUTTING PILE OR NAP FABRICS

A one-way fabric layout is needed when cutting pile or nap fabrics. One-way fabric layouts are also used when cutting printed fabric with an obvious one-way design. Cutting yokes, collars, pocket details or cuffs in the opposite direction of the nap will result in a contrast look. (Refer to the section *Cutting Fabric Accurately* on page 75).

Lace

Lace is a netlike fabric constructed of thread. An openwork fabric, the holes can be formed by removing threads or fabric from a woven fabric or created as part of the lace. Lace is created when a thread is looped, twisted or braided to other threads independently from a backing fabric. Historically, linen, silk and metallic threads have been used in lace making.

Today's laces are used in all types of clothing, ranging from very casual to eveningwear. Lace can be used as a stand-alone fabric or in combination/layers with fashion fabrics.

Today, cotton and blended fibres are frequently used. Designs might be flat and simple, featuring metallic, raised threads, beading or embroidery. Usually loosely woven lace can be made with stretch yarn. All laces have a definite pattern, which must be taken into account when cutting and sewing. There are several types of lace, which vary by type and weight of thread, design and the base material upon which the thread is applied.

STUDIO TIP

When sewing with lace fabrics, select an invisible zip with 'lace tape' to help conceal the zip.

STUDIO TIP

Pile or napped fabrics are usually cut with the nap running towards the lower edge of the garment. When choosing direction of nap, cut all major pieces in the same direction. Cutting the nap in the up direction usually produces a different texture and more intense colour.

LININGS

A lining is the duplicate of a garment, constructed of a suitable lining fabric and subsequently sewn into the garment. Lining a garment adds body and durability to the outer garment, while providing a more attractive inside finish.

Today's mills have engineered new types of linings. The newest linings are created from microfibre, used to weave the traditional twill, lightweight interlock tricot or nylon-backed cotton fleece linings. The various weaves help make the garment easier to wear, enhance the overall look of the design, make the garment more breathable, and create warmth when needed.

STUDIO TIP Use cotton-wrapped polyester or mercerized cotton thread and a size 11/75 needle.

Guidelines for Selecting Linings

When selecting a lining fabric, match quality and suitability of the lining fabric to the design and fabric of the garment to be lined. Colour, texture and weight, fibre content, weave and finish of the fabric must be considered when selecting appropriate lining. Lining fabric is usually lighter in weight than the fashion fabric, preventing distortion of the finished garment.

Fabrics commonly used as linings include rayon acetate, 100 per cent polyester, 100 per cent cotton, 100 per cent nylon and 100 per cent silk. Blended fibres, including rayon/polyester, cotton/nylon, polyester/nylon and silk/polyester are also used. For example, a blouse with see-through printed fabric would be lined with one of the newest lightweight polyester/cotton interlock blends.

TABLE 2.1 Guidelines for Selecting Linings

LINING WEIGHT	TYPICAL FABRICS	QUALITIES	CARE TIPS
Lightweight linings used for suit jackets, coats, tailored trousers and skirts.	100 per cent cotton or polyester blend	Ravels and could pull apart at the seams.	Machine wash. Might require preshrinking and dry cleaning.
	100 per cent acetate	Smooth, slick finish. Ravels and could pull apart at the seams.	Dry-clean only.
	Polyester/rayon blend acetate	Smooth finish. Ravels and could pull apart at the seams.	Machine wash and dry-clean.
	Polyester crêpe	Strong and durable.	Machine wash and dry. Press at low temperature.
	Rayon or acetate crêpe-backed satin	Smooth and flexible, with a bit more body than acetate.	Dry-clean only.
Medium-weight linings used for lining bustier dresses or evening gowns.	Satin (polyester or acetate) or taffeta (acetate or polyester)	Adds body and maintains shape. Smooth and durable.	Machine wash polyester. Dry-clean acetate.

INTERFACINGS

Interfacing, like fashion fabric, is constructed using a variety of fibres and weaves. Interfacings must be compatible with the weight, hand and stretch of the fashion fabric. The purpose of interfacing is to maintain the shape of the garment and to add body to selected areas of the garment.

Guidelines for Selecting Interfacings

The choice of interfacing should not alter the weight of the fashion fabric or adversely affect the garment's final appearance. Interfacing is never to be selected by feel, because all properties change when the interfacing is combined with the fashion fabric. Select interfacing based on fibre content, weave, finish (press-on or sew-in), colour and weight. Table 2.2, on the next page, describes the five types of interfacing and gives guidelines for selecting the most appropriate interfacing to complement the appearance, durability, maintenance and comfort of a garment.

Fibre Content

Interfacings are manufactured of natural fibres (such as cotton) or manufactured fibres (such as nylon, polyester or rayon). Natural and manufactured fibres are blended in varying percentages in most interfacings. Interfacing content will continue to evolve because of emerging technology. Selecting an interfacing compatible with the fashion fabric ensures a finished garment with the desired standards of care, shrinkage and washability. Conversely, poorly selected interfacing can damage the fashion fabric. For example, 100 per cent nylon interfacing distorts spandex or stretch denim fabrics, and a nylon/polyester blend interfacing works with 100 per cent rayon, 100 per cent cotton and 100 per cent challis.

Weave

Interfacing is made using one of five weaving processes:

1 **Woven** – Woven interfacing fabrics have a warp and weft construction. Woven interfacings include various types of fabrics, such as lawn, batiste, net, siri, organdie and canvas. A wide selection of weights and colours are available.

2 **Weft** – Weft interfacing is a combination of a woven and knit process. The knit weave (tricot) is woven loosely in the weft direction; the warp direction is a traditional weave. Weft

interfacings have been used in the garment industry for several years and are being introduced in the home sewing market. Open-weave wefts are used primarily to reinforce coat and suit fronts. Tighter and lighter wefts are primarily used with silk and synthetics. Weft interfacings are rapidly replacing hair canvas.

3 **Weft insertion** – Weft insertion is a nonwoven interfacing with a weft insertion in the crossgrain. The nonwoven fibres are placed on the grain, and a tricot knit is woven loosely in the weft direction. A disadvantage of weft insertion interfacing is that it tears easily. *Note: The fashion industry does not use this interfacing because it does not meet standards of wearability.*

4 **Tricot knit** – Tricot interfacing is usually 100 per cent nylon warp knit and tends to be run resistant. It is lightweight and comfortable to the touch. Tricot knit interfacing, such as fusible tricot or 'easy knit,' is used with knits. Tricot knit interfacings stretch in all directions and are more flexible than other types of interfacing. The majority of knit interfacings are fusible.

STUDIO TIP

The fashion industry does not preshrink interfacing. All interfacings used in production sewing include polyester or nylon in the fibre content, to prevent shrinkage.

5 **Nonwoven** – Nonwoven interfacings are considered bonded fabrics. These interfacings are created by thermally bonding or heat pressing crosslaid fibres into a finished fabric, giving cross-section stretch and recovery, and they have a look and feel similar to woven fabric. Nonwoven interfacings range from very fine/transparent to firm, are available in a range of colours and are engineered to combine well with light- to medium-weight fabrics.

Each process is available as a sew-in or fusible form. Properties of the interfacing will change as soon as the interfacing and the fashion fabric are joined or fused. Table 2.2 is a useful reference guide for selecting interfacings.

Weight

Weight is a major factor for selecting interfacing. Weight refers to the texture, body or drape of the interfacing fabric. The type and blend of fibre and the amount and type of glue used create significant weight differences among interfacing fabrics.

STUDIO TIP

When cutting nonwoven interfacing, all pattern pieces must be laid out, following the grainline, to ensure the fabric and interfacing perform in the same manner as woven fabric with regard to grainline, crossgrain and bias.

TABLE 2.2 Five Popular Interfacings for Fashion Sewing

INTERFACING TYPE	COLOUR	FINISH	DESCRIPTION
Weft – polyester/ rayon blend	White and black	Fusible	Use for women's wear front jacket applications and with dress-weight fabrics. Offers a soft, lightly resilient, round hand.
Nonwoven – all-purpose polyester/ nylon	White and charcoal	Fusible	Has the same properties of a woven fabric, such as grain, crossgrain and bias. Works well with almost any fabric, especially 100 per cent rayon, shirting cottons and blends. Gives a softer tailoring hand. Has special glue designed for rayon and other hard-to-fuse fabrics
Tricot for knits 100 per cent nylon	White and black	Fusible	Has a unique softness and drapeability for a wide range of knit fabrics. It fuses easily and performs well on knit. NOTE: Most knitted garment designs don't require interfacing because they usually don't have collars and the necklines are finished with ribbing or binding.
100 per cent polyester tricot	White and black	Fusible	Made of very fine fibres in a non-stretch tricot weave and is soft, stable and sheer. Designed for sheers, georgettes, and very lightweight fabrics. Also a good choice for linens and silks.
100 per cent woven cotton	White and black	Fusible	An excellent woven fusible interfacing that can be used for a wide range of lightweight to medium-weight woven fabrics, including pure worsteds and blends. Not suitable for fine fabrics or 100 per cent filament synthetics, such as acetate and nylon. Must be preshrunk.

Fusible vs Non-fusible

Non-fusible, or sew-in interfacing, is fabric without any glue. Non-fusible interfacing is available in a variety of colours and weights. It is attached by machine basting or overlocking on to the fabric.

Fusible interfacing has a heat-sensitive adhesive on one side, which is pressed onto the fabric. Fusible interfacings react differently depending on the amount and type of glue distributed on the surface. For example, the number of glue dots and the size of the dots vary. A fine dot may be referred to as 30 mesh, and a larger dot may be referred to as 17 mesh. The 30 mesh contains a larger number of dots per inch and smaller dots, usually used with fine, lightweight fabric. The 17 mesh has larger and fewer dots and is usually used with heavy- to medium-weight fabrics. Widely spaced, large glue dots on some fusible interfacings can harden and spot the fashion fabric. Other glues react well with fabric, maintaining quality and adding the desired body to the finished garment.

It is important to test fusible interfacing with a small piece of the fashion fabric. Check that the interfacing is not too stiff or rigid. Also make sure that the glue does not show through the fabric surface.

Preshrinking Interfacing

The fashion industry does not preshrink interfacing. All interfacings used in the fashion industry include polyester or nylon in the fibre content. This is to ensure that no shrinkage of the interfacing occurs within the finished garment. For easy reference, the first four interfacings listed in Table 2.2 are from the fashion industry and do not need preshrinking. Therefore, preshrinking interfacing is not necessary if the recommended selection guidelines are followed.

Preshrinking is recommended for all interfacing without polyester or nylon fibres. To preshrink interfacing, carefully fold in half, wrong side to wrong side, and place it in hot water for about 20 minutes. Remove the interfacing from the water and lay it on a towel. Gently pat away all excess water and place the interfacing on an airy, dry surface until it is thoroughly dry. For finished garments that will be dry-cleaned, the interfacing can be steamed with an iron. Do not touch the iron to the interfacing fabric because it could result in distortion.

STUDIO TIPS

- Block fusing interfacing is the process of selecting all pattern pieces requiring interfacing. Calculate the amount of fabric the interfacing pieces will require. Precut this amount from the fashion fabric. Using the same amount of interfacing, steam and press the interfacing to the wrong side of the fashion fabric. Cut the fabric and the interfacing at the same time. The pieces will not distort.
- Fuse interfacing to wrong side of fabric, then cut pattern pieces that require interfacing.

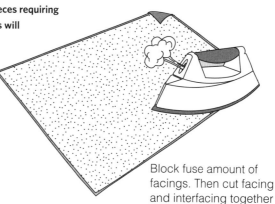

Block fuse amount of facings. Then cut facing and interfacing together

Attaching Fusible Interfacing

Fusible interfacing is applied through the process of bonding/fusing. Most irons have a temperature range from cool to hot. If an iron is too cold, it might not fuse the interfacing. Test the iron temperature with a small swatch of the garment fabric and interfacing.

1 Cut the interfacing. Place the coated side of the interfacing piece to the wrong side of the garment area to be interfaced.

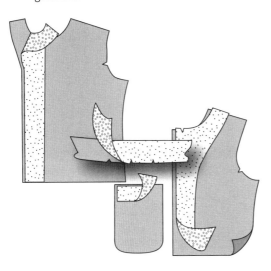

3 Clean finish the outer edge of the facing piece. Use an overlocker, a machine zigzag stitch, or fold 6mm of the outer edge of the facing over the interfacing.

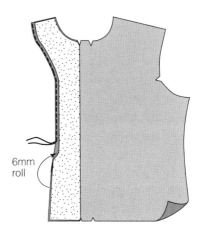

6mm roll

2 Using a steam iron, press the interfacing to the fabric by lifting the iron and steaming a section at a time. If the interfacing does not adhere to the fabric, use a damp pressing cloth between the iron and the interfacing to create more steam. Continue to use the steam setting on the iron and add pressure.

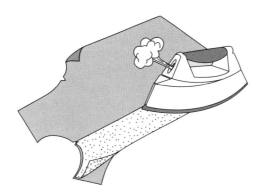

STUDIO TIPS

- If the interfacing has stiffened the finish of the garment pieces, the amount of glue is wrong for the fabric. Another interfacing should be selected with less glue.
- If the interfacing does not adhere to the fabric, this means that there was not enough steam and pressure applied when pressing the interfacing to the fabric. Use a damp pressing cloth between the iron and the interfacing to create more steam. Or better yet, use a steam-generated iron. Continue to use the steam setting on the iron and add pressure. Heat and steam will melt the glue onto the fashion fabric. If the glue does not melt, the interfacing will not adhere to the garment.

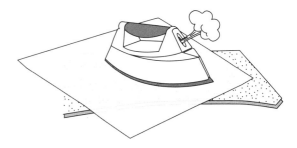

Attaching Non-fusible Interfacings

Non-fusible interfacing, or sew-in interfacing, does not have any glue. It is attached by machine basting or overlocking it to the garment.

1 Cut the interfacing. Pin the interfacing to the wrong side of the garment or facing, placing the edge of the interfacing along the outer edge of the garment section.

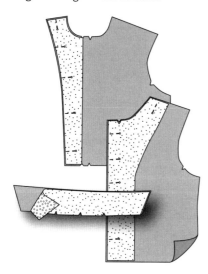

2 Machine stitch 6mm from the outer edge.

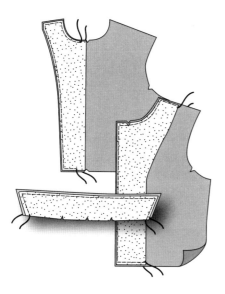

3 Machine or catch stitch the loose edge of the interfacing to the wrong side of the fabric if necessary.

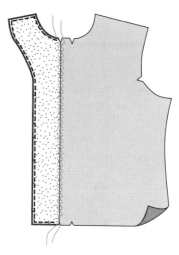

4 Clean finish the outer edge of the facing. Use an overlocker/serger, a machine zigzag stitch, or fold 6mm of the outer edge of the facing over the interfacing.

- Fold the edge of the garment detail over the interfacing.
- Then use a small hand-hemming stitch, machine overlock or zigzag stitch to reduce bulk.

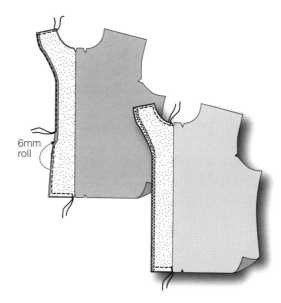

6mm roll

CHAPTER

3

BODY TYPES *and* SIZE CHARTS

- Understanding Body Types

- Women

- Children

- Adolescents

- Men

UNDERSTANDING BODY TYPES

Understanding body types is important before selecting a pattern size. Body type describes the height and shape of an individual. The following illustrations and charts represent the various body types for women, children and men. All measurements are in metric.

After you identify a body type, take accurate measurements to determine the pattern size needed. Underclothes or a leotard should be worn while taking measurements; shoes should not be worn. For a reference point, tie a piece of twill tape around the waistline. Measure and record the circumference of the bust, waist and hips (fullest part). Also measure the length of the centre back, neck to waist and the sleeve.

WOMEN
Juniors, 1.63m to 1.65m (5'4" to 5'5")
Small frame, short figure and small proportions. Usually a young adult.

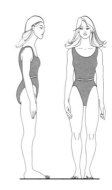

(MEASUREMENTS IN CM)						
Pattern & retail size	3–4	5–6	7–8	9–10	11–12	13–14
Bust	71	73.5	77.5	81	85	89
Waist	56	58.5	61	63.5	66	68.5
Hips	78.5	81	85	89	92.5	96.5
Back waist length	34	35.5	37	38	39.5	40

Misses, 1.65m to 1.68m (5'5" to 5'6")
Fully developed, well-proportioned figure, longer waist length, fuller bust and hips, but generally slim.

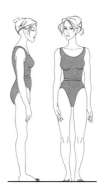

(MEASUREMENTS IN CM)						
Pattern & retail size	6	8	10	12	14	16
Bust	78	80	83	87	92	97
Waist	58	61	64	67	71	76
Hips	83	85	88	92	97	102
Back waist length	39.5	40	40.5	41.5	42	42.5

Full-figured Women, 1.65m to 1.68m (5'5" to 5'6")

A fuller-figured woman with the same proportions as the misses figure. Usually the waist and bust are thicker and heavier.

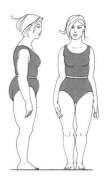

(MEASUREMENTS IN CM)							
Pattern size	38	40	42	44	46	48	50
Bust	107	112	117	122	127	132	137
Waist	89	94	99	105	112	118	124
Hips	112	117	122	127	132	137	142
Back waist length	44	44	44.5	45	45	45.5	46

Shorter Women, 1.52m to 1.68m (5' to 5'6")

More mature, short-waisted woman with a shorter, heavier body type. This is usually a woman who has gone through menopause.

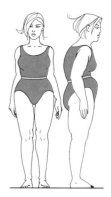

(MEASUREMENTS IN CM)						
Pattern size	38	40	42	44	46	48
Bust	107	112	117	122	127	132
Waist	89	94	99	105	112	118
Hips	112	117	122	127	132	137
Back waist length	41	42	42	42.5	42.5	43

CHILDREN

Children's wear is usually sized by the age of the child. However, because children do not grow at the same pace, some children may reach a certain size earlier or later, depending on the rate of growth and development. Therefore, the child must be measured often and those measurements compared to the listing on the pattern. All measurements here are in metric.

Infants

Newborn infant to 18 months. Sizes are determined by the baby's weight and height. Usually the styles for boys and girls are similar.

Pattern size	NEWBORN–3 MOS X-SMALL	3–6 MOS SMALL	6–12 MOS MEDIUM	12–18 MOS LARGE
Weight (kg)	5.4	6–7	7–8	8.5–9.5
Height (cm)	61	64–66	69–74	74–76

infant

Toddlers

Sizes for boys and girls are the same, but the designs vary slightly.

Pattern size	1	2	3	4
Height	79	87	94	102
Chest	51	53	56	58
Waist	50	51	52	53

toddler

Little Girls

Children's patterns are designed for a young child who is walking and not wearing nappies.

Pattern size	4	5	6	6X
Height	104	112	119	122
Chest	58	61	64	65
Waist	53	55	56	57
Hips	61	64	66	67

little girl

Little Boys

Children's patterns are designed for a young child who is walking and not wearing nappies.

Pattern size	4	5	6	6X
Height	104	112	119	122
Chest	58	61	64	65
Waist	53	55	56	57
Hips	61	64	66	67

little boy

Older Girls

Girls are shorter than teen girls, with less developed figures. This size is for girls at the beginning of a growth period that usually represents awkward proportions and styles are more trendy.

Pattern size	7	8	10	12	14
Height	127	132	142	149	155
Chest	66	69	73	76	81
Waist	58	60	62	65	67
Hips	69	71	76	81	87

older girl

Older Boys

Boys' styles are patterned after men's clothing. However, some boys' trouser styles include slim and chubby variations.

Pattern size	8	10	12	14	16
Height	132	142	149	155	156
Chest	69	73	76	81	87
Waist	60	62	65	67	70
Hips	71	76	81	87	92

older boy

ADOLESCENTS
Teen Boys, 155cm to 173cm

Teen boys are usually between boys' and men's sizes. The preppy look is most often a choice for this age group. (Measurements in cm).

Pattern size	10	12	14	16	18	20
Neck	32	33	34.5	35.5	37	38
Chest	71	76	81	85	89	93
Waist	64	66	69	71	74	76
Hip	75	79	83	87	90	94

Young Juniors/Teen Girls, 132cm to 161cm

Young juniors/teen girls have very small busts, thick waists and fairly small hips. (Measurements in cm).

Pattern size	8½	10½	12½	14½	16½
Bust	76	80	84	88	92
Waist	71	74	76	79	81
Hips	84	88	92	96	96
Back waist	32	34	35.5	37.5	39.5

MEN
Men, 1.73m to 1.83m (5'8" to 6')

Most men's patterns are designed for men of average build about 1.78m tall without shoes. Sizes for men's suits, jackets and sports shirts are based on the chest measurement. Dress shirts are based on the neck and sleeve measurements. Trousers are sized by the waist measurement. (Measurements in cm).

Men's Sport Shirts, Dress Shirts and Trousers

Pattern size	34	36	38	40	42	44	46	48
Neck	35.5	37	38	39.5	40.5	42	43	44.5
Chest	87	92	97	102	107	112	117	122
Waist	71	76	81	87	92	99	107	112
Sleeve length	81	81	84	84	87	87	89	89

PLANNING A DESIGN *and* SELECTING FABRIC

- Planning a Design
- Selecting a Pattern
- Fitting the Pattern
- Pattern and Fabric Layout
- Transferring Pattern Markings

PLANNING A DESIGN

Selecting Fashion Fabric

The first step in creating designs is to examine the body proportions along with the colour and fabric palette. Create styles that will reflect your social and artistic forces. The designs created give immediate communication about the wearer to everyone they meet. The clothes should not only be attractive to others but should instil confidence. To achieve these goals, it is important to make clothes that complement and flatter the shape of the body. Identify what pleases and works. There are many aspects of a figure where one can create the perfect illusion with style and colour.

DESIGN FEATURES: Emphasizing the best features of the body is the most important guideline in selecting a design. If the bustline is the best characteristic of a body, design plain bodices with draped effects and/or bright, shiny fabrics. If the bust cup is smaller, designs with added fullness above the waist can be worn. For a small waist and large hips, do not overemphasize the waistline with bright or gaudy belts. Use thinner, plain belts when necessary for the design. Tall women can easily wear any width of belt. For large hips, darker colours for skirts will make the hips appear smaller.

DESIGN LINES: Unbroken design lines are used to create illusions. For example, use princess seams, elongated collars, vertical tucks, vertical pleats, vertical lace trims or elongated front openings to create the appearance of being taller or thinner. For jackets, the finished hem should be at wrist level, unless it is a short-cropped jacket. Full skirts can be worn by thinner figures or those needing to minimize hip lines. Gored skirts flatter any figure, with the length of the skirt varying according to the wearer's height. Empire design creates a longer leg line and height. To avoid a 'top heavy' look, the hem sweep should equal the width of the hip and shoulder line.

SELECTING FABRIC QUALITY: It is important to select the right quality of fabric for the design. Natural fibres, such as cotton, linen, silk and wool, breathe with the body, making the garments more pleasant to wear. Softer fabrics minimize and soften the body's appearance. These fabrics also drape in vertical folds, slenderizing and lengthening the figure. Rough, shiny or stiff fabrics, if used for an entire garment, will accentuate the figure and create a flattering silhouette. Combining rough, shiny or stiff fabrics with softer fabrics adds style interest.

SELECTING FABRIC WEIGHT: In creating designs that are the best for the figure, there are a few guidelines that should be followed. For instance, thin fabrics subtract inches and heavier fabrics add inches. Also, solid colours enhance design details, whereas plaids and prints make the design detail less noticeable. Dark colours minimize the figure. Fabrics with vertical lines help create the illusion of being thinner, whereas wide stripes can make the figure look heavier.

SELECTING PRINT FABRICS: Overall prints with soft, misty shapes best complement a figure; this print style can be dramatic or simple. Current popular prints that flatter the figure include the following designs: geometric, graphic, garden, floral, polka dots and stripes. Creating a wardrobe using mix-and-match fabrics or positive/negative prints adds style to the garment and creates a thinner silhouette.

COLOUR PREFERENCE: Developing and personalizing a design requires careful use of colour. Colour represents purpose and evokes emotion. A pleasing blend of colour, fabric and design can produce a flattering garment to present the positive characteristics of the body.

Neutral colours (black, brown, grey, beige) visually minimize an area, whereas lighter, brighter colours attract attention. Garments made of one continuous colour (or monochromatic blend) generate a long, slenderizing appearance. Dressing in black requires simple lines, perfect cuts and a touch of creativity. The little black dress is not only an indispensable item in any wardrobe, it is also an ideal choice for any occasion.

Colours should flow from head to toe to create the maximum illusion of height. Used properly, colour contrast can balance the body proportions and de-emphasize figure flaws. Place neutral and darker colours in areas to be minimized and lengthened. Highlight areas near the face and the best features by using bright, eye-catching colours.

Preshrinking Fabric

When heat or steam is applied to fabric, the threads relax and shrink. Many fabrics shrink when washed or dry-cleaned. Common fabrics possessing high degrees of shrinkage include: untreated 100 per cent cotton, linen and wool. It is important to preshrink many fabrics to prevent altering the size of a garment after washing or dry-cleaning.

TABLE 4.1 Preshrinking Fabric Chart

FABRIC	METHOD
100 per cent cotton, untreated	Place fabric in washing machine on the spin cycle, which adds a minimum of water without soaking the fabric. Remove the fabric from the washer and place it in an automatic dryer. The heat shrinks the damp fabric. Remove from dryer when completely dry.
100 per cent wool, untreated	Take the fabric to a dry-cleaner and request the fabric be steamed and pressed only. No cleaning is needed. The heat from the steam process relaxes the threads and shrinks the fabric.
100 per cent linen, untreated	Use either the washer/dryer or dry-cleaning method described above. The dry-cleaning method is simpler, because untreated 100 per cent linen wrinkles.
Silk, rayon, polyester and other synthetic blended fabrics	No preshrinking needed.

Blocking

Blocking ensures that lengthwise and crossgrain threads are at right angles to each other. A finished sewn garment must hang correctly. Therefore, it is important to check the fabric before cutting to determine whether the crossgrain threads are distorted. To block fabric that is distorted, fold the fabric selvedge to selvedge, pin all the fabric edges together (excluding the folded side), tack the grainline to a board or table, and gently pull on the crossgrain threads until all the threads are at a 90-degree angle.

STUDIO TIPS

- When fabric is produced at the mill, to maintain perfect grain and crossgrain, the finished rolls are laid down on pallets for shipping. Each manufacturer stores the rolls lying down. When the fabric is laid down for cutting, the rolls are placed on a 'spreader' that has tension bars to maintain straightness of grain and crossgrain. Because the grain and crossgrain have not been distorted, there is no need to block the fabric.

- Fabric grain is distorted when the fabric has been folded in half and placed on a bolt. The bolt is then displayed in the fabric shop standing on end. How much the fabric has been pulled off grain depends on how long the bolt has been displayed in this manner. Many fine woollens are sold 'needle ready', meaning that the fabric has been treated and is ready for cutting and sewing. The newer, washable wools might not require pretreating with heat and steam.

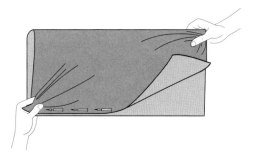

Selecting the Fabric for the Designed Garment

For a successful finished garment, it is important to select a fabric that matches sewing skill level. Plaids, one-way fabrics, heavy or very lightweight fabrics, sequined, pile and stretch fabrics all require a higher level of sewing skill. Broadcloth, cotton polyester blends, cotton, linen and medium-weight wool are suitable for those with basic sewing skills. When selecting fabric, carefully drape a yard or more over the arm, holding the fabric next to the body.

The following chart lists categories of garments, the fabrics most often used for these categories, and care requirements. The information is arranged by difficulty, with the simplest type of design and the least-difficult-to-handle fabric listed first, progressing to increasingly complex designs and more difficult-to-handle fabrics.

TABLE 4.2 Guide to Selecting Fabrics

GARMENT CATEGORY	TYPICAL FABRICS	CARE REQUIREMENTS
Sportswear, warm-weather clothes, casual day dresses, skirts, trousers, men's dress shirts, play clothes.	Medium-weight woven or knit. 100 per cent cotton, corduroy, denim, poplin, seersucker, broadcloth, pique, flannel, chamois, oxford cloth.	Machine wash. Cotton shrinks unless preshrunk or treated. Very durable. Allows for good air circulation. Press while damp or with a hot iron.
	Medium-weight woven or knit cotton/polyester. Medium-weight wool or wool flannel.	Machine wash. Does not shrink. May use bleach. Press with hot steam iron. Woollens must be dry-cleaned unless labelled washable.
	Medium-weight linen or challis.	Wrinkles; tends to shrink when machine washed. Dry-clean. Stretches when wet if not preshrunk.
	Open weave cottons. Monk's cloth, homespun and gauze.	Machine wash. Shrinks unless preshrunk.
Active sportswear, swimwear, costumes and speciality clothes, such as Lycra trousers and knits.	Stretch knits. Spandex.	Machine wash. Dry at low temperature. Do not bleach. Press with cool iron.
	Woven cotton/polyester.	Machine wash. Does not shrink. Dries quickly. Little or no ironing.
Tailored jackets, medium-weight to heavier weight coats, suits and sports coats.	Heavyweight hair blends. Wool, cashmere, camel, alpaca, wool tweed, cheviot.	Dry-clean only, unless otherwise instructed. Some wool is now labelled washable.
	Heavy woven cottons. Denim and duck.	Machine wash. Shrinks unless preshrunk or treated.
	Medium-weight to heavier weight linen, blended fabrics, silks, rayons, sueded fabrics.	Dry-clean only, unless otherwise instructed.
	Heavyweight or medium-weight leather and fake fur.	Speciality dry-clean. Also requires special seam construction.
	Nylon or quilted nylon with an inner layer of down or polyester fibre fill.	Machine wash or dry-clean. Needs little or no ironing.

TABLE 4.2 Guide to Selecting Fabrics

Sleepwear, intimate apparel, blouses and better dresses.	Sheer cottons. Batiste, dotted swiss, lawn, voile, and gauze.	Machine wash. Shrink unless preshrunk or treated. Wrinkles easily. Press while damp or with a steam iron.
	Sheer to lightweight fabrics. 100 per cent polyester or polyester blends, georgette, chiffon, organza, poly/silk.	Machine wash. Needs little or no ironing.
	Lightweight to medium-weight fabrics. Fleeces, flannel, silk, satin, shantung, rayon, crêpe de Chine, rayon, knits.	
	Dry-clean only, unless otherwise instructed. Many new fabrics, fleece, flannel and blends are machine washable.	
Evening dresses and evening jackets.	Sheer to lightweight fabrics. Organza, chiffon, organdy, transparent cotton, silk, rayon, blended fabrics, lamé, sheer laces.	Dry-clean only, unless otherwise instructed.
	Lightweight to medium-weight fabrics. Raw silk, satin, taffeta, brocade, velvet, velveteen, lightweight wool (challis, flannel, crêpe jersey), metallic fabrics, heavier laces, beaded fabrics.	

SELECTING A PATTERN

Selecting the Correct Size

The pattern can be selected first, with the purchase of fabric as suggested on the pattern envelope, or the fabric can be purchased followed by pattern selection suitable for the fabric. Those who are able to visualize the completed garment tend to use the latter method. The pattern envelope, discussed in greater detail in this chapter, provides a list of suggested fabrics for garments included in the pattern.

Before purchasing a pattern, measure the person for whom the garment is being made and determine their body type. (Refer to Chapter 3 for Body Types and Size Charts.)

WOMEN

- Use the full bust measurement to select the correct pattern size for a blouse, shirt, jacket or dress.
- Use the hip measurement (widest part) to select the correct pattern size for trousers or a skirt.

CHILDREN

- Use the chest measurement to select the correct pattern size for a shirt or blouse.
- Use the waist measurement to select the correct pattern size for a skirt or trouser pattern.

MEN

- Use the chest measurement to select the correct pattern size for suits, jackets and shirts.
- Use the neck circumference and sleeve length measurements to select the correct pattern size for dress shirts.
- Use the waist measurement to select the correct pattern size for trousers.

HIGH BUST VERSUS FULL BUST

Patterns are developed by using the full bust of the model. If the high bust measurement is used to determine the pattern size, the pattern will be too small for the customer and the side seam/armhole will need to be reworked. This results in an unbalanced armhole, making the sleeve hang incorrectly and/or pull. Custom fit the shoulder/neckline for distance, slant and width. (See fitting on pages 70–74.)

Understanding a Pattern Envelope

Pattern envelopes vary from company to company. The following example illustrates the various features and information included on pattern envelopes.

Size range

The size range notes the sizes that are included in the envelope.

Fashion illustration or photographs of the design

In most cases, patterns are included for all the designs illustrated on the envelope. If a garment is not included, it will be clearly noted.

Level of difficulty

Some pattern envelopes also advise on the sewing skill required to successfully complete the garment. Beginners should choose 'Easy-to-Sew' patterns, whereas experienced sewers might choose 'Designer' or 'Advanced' patterns.

Pattern description

This area describes all the styling details of each design. It might also describe the overall fit of each garment (loose, semi-fitted, fitted, and so on). Keep in mind that you can change simple details such as the pocket styling or collar outer edge styling.

Suggested fabrics

The fabrics suggested exhibit particular drape and hand qualities that are best suited for the specific design. The pattern envelope will indicate if the pattern is suitable for knit fabrics.

Company sizing specifications

These specifications describe the body size and figure type that the pattern is designed to fit. If your measurements vary from the standard sizing, look for a finished measurements section printed on the envelope or on the actual pattern pieces. Most likely, some alterations will need to be made. Refer to the pattern fitting section in this chapter.

Fabric amount required

The fabric amount required is displayed for each design included in the pattern. Fabric amounts are traditionally provided for 115cm (45in) and 150cm (60in) wide fabrics.

NOTE: The English section displays imperial numbering requirements; the French section displays metric requirements.

Notions required

Necessary sewing notions such as buttons, zips, hooks, elastic, thread and so on, are listed for each garment.

Finished garment measurements

Finished lengths and hem circumferences for trousers, skirts and dresses are especially helpful for estimating the fullness of a design and whether length alterations will need to be made. Finished measurements, when included, are useful for estimating the fitting ease of each garment. These measurements are usually found on the pattern pieces for the front bust/chest, waist and full hip.

Flat sketches

Flat sketches are line drawings of the pattern style details. These are useful when pattern details are difficult to see in the front envelope illustrations or photographs. Some pattern companies display only sketches of the back view; others display both the front and back views. In this case, the flat sketches are on the front of the envelope. Where the flat sketches appear on the package depends on the manufacturer's layout policies.

INSIDE THE PATTERN ENVELOPE

Pattern pieces printed on tissue paper and a pattern guide sheet are included inside the envelope. The size, style number, and/or letter are printed on each pattern piece.

The guide sheet illustrates suggested pattern layouts on a variety of fabric widths, styles, and sizes (see 'Pattern and Fabric Layout,' pages 75–80). There might be additional layouts for 'napped' or one-way fabrics, including velvet, corduroy satin, plaid, uneven stripes or one-way prints.

The guide sheet also provides step-by-step sewing instructions for sewing the design selected.

NOTE: See Fitting the Pattern on pages 70–74, to custom fit the pattern pieces before laying out and cutting the design.

Identifying Markings

Pattern markings enable the manufacturer to convey information about the construction of a garment to the sewer. Some markings are accompanied by written instructions, often in several languages.

Identifying Pattern Notches

A notch is a mark or set of marks (cross marks) placed on a pattern to indicate the position where corresponding pattern/garment areas are to be matched for sewing or gathering. You should always be able to identify the following notches and markings on a pattern:

- Grainline
- Centre front (c.f.)
- Centre back (c.b.)
- Darts, tucks and pleats
- Shoulder markings
- All fold lines
- Single notch in front armhole
- Double notch in back armhole
- Pocket positions
- Alteration lines

Seam Allowances

Seam allowances are added to any edge that is to be joined to another edge. Some pattern companies have added the seam allowances, whereas others leave the patterns without seam allowances. If the pattern is custom made or a pattern is used without seam allowances, it will be necessary to add them to enable the garment pieces to be sewn together. To simplify how much seam allowance is to be used, add 12 or 16mm to all outer edges. For custom patterns, it is recommended that a 6mm seam be added to all enclosed seams, such as necklines, collars, and facing edges instead of a 12 or 16mm seam.

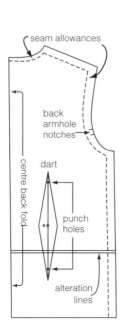

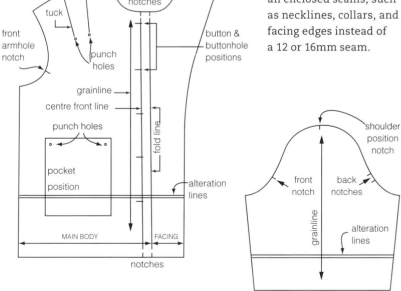

FITTING *the* PATTERN

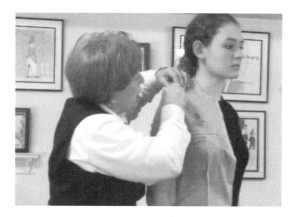

After the pattern design and size have been selected, a preliminary fitting should be completed to check the size and fit of the pattern and make any necessary adjustments.

Illustrated here are fitting guidelines learned during 35 years in the fashion industry. These simple draping techniques can be applied to almost any pattern with excellent results. Drape-fitting the pattern enables custom changes and gives added visual pleasure in how the style fits.

It is important to have an appropriately fitting garment. All pattern areas have a definite relationship with the figure that enables the garment to be worn and fit correctly. These areas include:

- Centre front and centre back of the garment should always be vertical to the floor and hang straight up and down.
- The grainline of the garment should be parallel to the centre front and centre back. If not, the garment will twist or pull.
- The crossgrain of the pattern should always be parallel to the floor. Otherwise the garment will drag and pull downwards.
- Garments hang from the shoulder and bust/chest. These pattern areas must be identical to the body shape. If the pattern shoulder slope is off just five degrees from the body shoulder slope, the garment will drape incorrectly.
- The armholes should fit comfortably according to the design (shirt armholes are larger than fitted armholes) and the neckline should lie flat against the body.

Preparing the Pattern

To check the fit and make pattern changes, follow these simple steps. Because the patterns are made on the half, only one half of the body will be fitted. Fit the pattern over tight-fitting clothing, a leotard or a dress form.

1 **SELECT PATTERN PIECES:** Remove the main front, back and sleeve pieces from the pattern package. For added stability and easy fitting, fuse the back side of the pattern pieces to a press-on nonwoven interfacing. Match the grainlines of the pattern pieces to the grain of the interfacing. Trim the pattern pieces to the size selected. Do not remove the seam allowances. Clip the neckline and armholes to the stitchline.

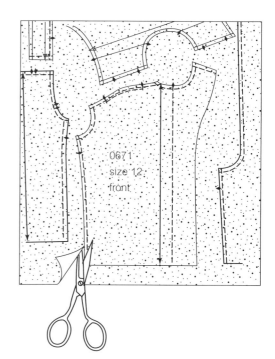

STUDIO TIP To give the pattern pieces added stability, press the back side of the pattern pieces to a press-on nonwoven interfacing. This technique gives enough body to the pattern to be able to accurately drape and fit the pattern pieces without sewing a toile/muslin.

2 DRAW THE GRAINLINE AND CROSSGRAIN LINES:

- On the front and back pieces, draw the centre front line and the centre back line.
- On the front pattern, draw a perfect crossgrain line at the bust level.
- On the back pattern, draw a perfect crossgrain at the shoulder blade level – 13mm below the neckline.

3 CHECK THE PATTERN SIDE SEAM BALANCE:
Pin side seams together at the underarm/side seam corner (before the shoulder seams are pinned). At this pinned location, pivot the pattern until the centre front and centre back are parallel. The side seams should match and be the same shape and length. If they are not, divide the difference to make them the same (see illustration).

4 CHECK THE PATTERN FOR FRONT TO BACK BALANCE:
The front pattern piece should be 13mm wider than the back pattern. When the side seams are pinned together (before the shoulder seams are pinned), the centre front and centre back should be parallel. At the same time, the side seams should be the same shape and length (refer to Step 3).

5 CHECK THE ARMHOLE BALANCE:
To ensure that the sleeve will hang correctly, the armholes should be balanced and shaped correctly. The back armhole distance should be 13mm longer than the front armhole measurement. If the distance is quite a bit off – more than 19mm – then a fitting is necessary, especially in the back shoulder area.

- Measure the front armhole.
- Measure the back armhole.

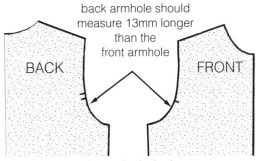

back armhole should measure 13mm longer than the front armhole

BACK   FRONT

check armhole balance

6 PIN THE PATTERN PIECES TOGETHER:
Pin together the side seams, all style lines and darts. Because most patterns are made on the half, only one half of the body will be fitted with the pattern. Pin the blouse front and blouse back together, matching perfectly the shoulder seams and side seams. Do not include facings, collars or sleeves (unless raglan style or kimono style) in the fitting. Do not pin the shoulders yet.

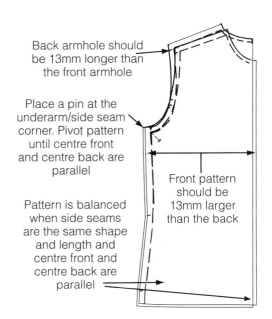

Back armhole should be 13mm longer than the front armhole

Place a pin at the underarm/side seam corner. Pivot pattern until centre front and centre back are parallel

Pattern is balanced when side seams are the same shape and length and centre front and centre back are parallel

Front pattern should be 13mm larger than the back

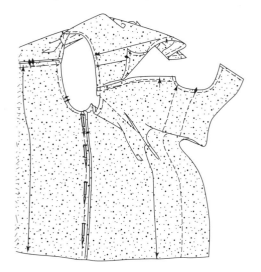

7 DRAPE-FIT THE PATTERN: Because the patterns are made on the half, only one half of the body will be fitted. Fit the pattern over tight-fitting clothing or a leotard. Place the prepared pattern over the body or a custom dress form. Fit the following areas:

ALIGN CENTRE FRONT AND CENTRE BACK: Align centre front, centre back and the side seam until the pattern hangs perfectly plumb, straight up and down. Make sure the pattern is not twisting or pitching toward the front or back. Use the backbone as the guide for centre back and use the belly button as the guide for centre front. The shoulder seams are not pinned at this time.

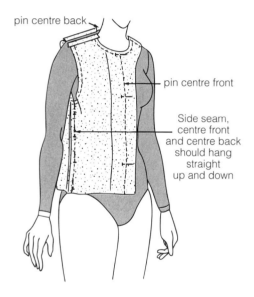

pin centre back

pin centre front

Side seam, centre front and centre back should hang straight up and down

SIDE SEAM FIT: Check for the proper amount of side seam shape and ease. All garments should have some ease for body movement. The amount will depend on the style of the garment. Readjust the side seam ease by adding to or taking in the side seam over the hip, waist and underarm areas.

SHOULDER FIT: Smooth the pattern from the mid-armhole area up to the shoulder, until the shoulder and neckline areas lie flat. If the shoulder seams do not meet, add paper extensions to the shoulder seams until they meet. The desired shoulder width should be marked at this time.

BUST DARTS: Bust darts should point to the fullest part of the bust. Crossmark this point and redraw a new dart from the widest part of the dart to the new crossmark.

PRINCESS SEAMS: For a smaller bust cup, remove any excess 'cupping' from the side front panel, as illustrated. If a larger bust cup is needed, add more fullness between the notches of the side front panel.

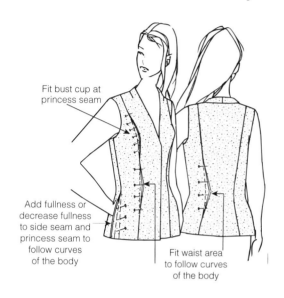

Fit bust cup at princess seam

Add fullness or decrease fullness to side seam and princess seam to follow curves of the body

Fit waist area to follow curves of the body

REMINDER: Garments hang from the shoulder. These areas must be identical to the body for correct fit and drape. If the pattern shoulder slope is off just five degrees from your shoulder slope, the garment will drape incorrectly.

Drape back shoulder area up to the shoulder seam. Repin new shoulder fit. Draw a new back neckline and armhole

Garment should hang straight from the shoulder blade level

ARMHOLE ADJUSTMENT: Most patterns are made for an average bicep. A smaller or larger armhole may be desired. For a smaller armhole, raise the side seam/armhole corner and reblend to the notches. For a larger armhole, lower the side seam/armhole corner and reblend to the notches. After the armhole is changed, simply select a smaller or larger sleeve that fits into the armhole. See illustration.

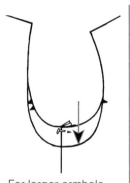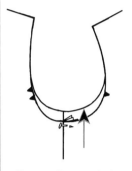

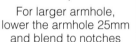

| For larger armhole, lower the armhole 25mm and blend to notches | For smaller armhole, raise the armhole 25mm and blend to notches |

8 **MARK THE FITTED PATTERN:** Using a soft pencil or felt-tip pen, mark all fitting adjustments. Unpin the pattern and lay it flat. Redraw any newly marked lines with a ruler and add new seam allowances to the adjusted areas. Cut and sew the pattern using an inexpensive fabric to check the sleeve fit.

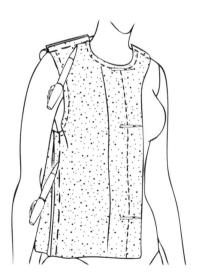

FINAL SLEEVE FIT: After the correct armhole size is determined, the sleeve can be fitted. Cut the sleeve out of muslin or an inexpensive fabric. Baste-stitch or hand-sew the sleeve into the armhole, matching all notches. Be sure to match the shoulder position mark to the shoulder seam. This mark controls the hang of the sleeve. Make the following changes if problems occur.

- Sleeve cap too short – add cap distance by blending from the notches to the desired amount needed at the cap.
- Sleeve twists – add 12–25mm at the back sleeve cap. Reblend the back sleeve cap from the back sleeve notches to the shoulder seam mark.
- Sleeve movement is restricted – adjust the underarm by lifting the underarm/side seam up 25mm and out 13mm and blend it back into the cap 25mm above the notches.

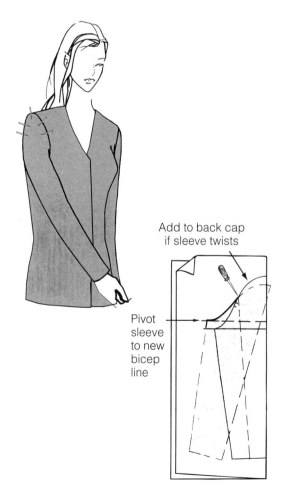

Add to back cap if sleeve twists

Pivot sleeve to new bicep line

SKIRT WAISTLINE FITTING: As women mature, their waistlines will tilt up or down in the front. To make sure the skirt hemlines are parallel to the floor, it is best to shape the waistlines to match the body slope.

- Using the pattern size that matches the hip measurement, add 25mm along the top waistline area seam. Cut and sew the main skirt pieces to make a complete skirt. Do not finish the waistline.
- Place the skirt on the body, correct side out of fabric. Tie a piece of twill tape or 6mm-wide elastic around the waistline. Adjust the waist area (pulling up or down above the twill tape) until the hemline and hip level are parallel to the floor.
- Adjust any darts or pleats smaller or larger to fit the waistline.
- Draw the new waistline. Transfer these markings to the pattern.

TROUSER FITTING AREAS: Because of a variety of figure types and crotch depths, it is recommended that a trouser be fitted in inexpensive fabric before making it in fashion fabric.

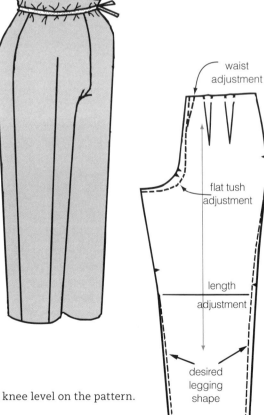

- Use the pattern size that matches the hip measurement. On the pattern, add 25mm along the top waistline area seam. Cut the pattern out of test fabric. Sew the crotch seams, side seams and inseams. Pin any dart or pleats. Press the trousers with the legging crease. Place the trousers on the body, correct side out.
- Tie a piece of twill tape or 6mm-wide elastic around the waistline. Position the trouser waistline area up or down until the crotch is in a comfortable position and the hip level is parallel to the floor. The trousers should drape up and down with no twisting. (This method adjusts the crotch depth in addition to fine-tuning the waist shape.)
- Pin the darts and pleats smaller or larger to fit the waistline. If the waistline amount is changed, adjust the waistband to match the new waistline.
- Draw the new waistline at the twill tape. Transfer these markings to the pattern.
- If the back crotch has too much fullness or it sags, sew a deeper curve in the back crotch area.
- Determine the trouser length. Adjust this amount at the knee level on the pattern.

waist adjustment

flat tush adjustment

length adjustment

desired legging shape

PATTERN *and* FABRIC LAYOUT

Cutting Fabric Accurately

The fabric has been selected, the pattern has been fitted, and it is time to place the pattern pieces on to fashion fabric. Taking time to cut with care and accuracy will save time and trouble later on and will result in a better-looking garment. It is important to create a layout that works well with the fabric. (See layout guidelines on the following pages.)

GETTING A TRUE CUT

Stabilizing all fabric with brown craft paper, shelf paper, butcher paper or unprinted newsprint ensures that the fabric will not slip, distort or move during cutting. This is especially vital when cutting lightweight fabrics, such as rayon, linings, chiffon, silk, crêpe, knit or velvet. Cutting with a paper support also helps achieve a clean, more accurate cut, and it will not dull fabric scissors or rotary cutters any more than normal use.

NOTE: The fashion industry requires cutting with paper because absolute accuracy is demanded.

1 Place a sheet of paper (brown craft paper, shelf paper, butcher paper or unprinted newsprint) on the cutting surface. On the paper, draw a crossgrain line perfectly perpendicular to the paper/ selvedge edge. Keeping the fabric flat and smooth, align and pin the fabric (single layer or folded) to the paper edge and crossgrain line. This ensures perfect lengthwise and crosswise grain alignment. The entire length of fabric can be pinned in place. If you run out of table space, gently fold up the pinned sections until the entire piece is pinned in place.

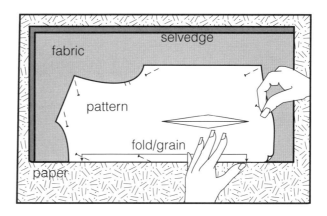

2 Press the pattern pieces with a dry iron to remove any creases. Pin all 'place on fold' pieces first. Lay out all other pieces, aligning grainlines first, until the entire layout is complete. Pin the remaining pieces to the fabric and paper support.

3 Cut the paper, fabric and pattern all at the same time. Use long, continuous strokes to eliminate jagged edges. Do not make short, 'choppy' cuts. Notice that the fabric does not move as the scissors cut. The pinned fabric piece can also be moved and adjusted closer to the cutter without distorting the fabric.

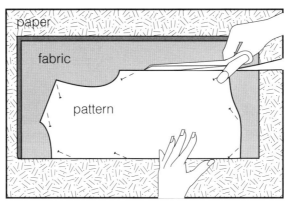

cut paper, fabric and pattern at the same time

Selecting Pattern Layout

As discussed previously, every pattern company provides a guide sheet to illustrate the particular pattern layouts for various fabric widths, styles and sizes. There may also be versions of the layouts for nap fabrics, which have pile or brushed surfaces, such as velvet, corduroy and one-way prints. These layouts must be followed very carefully. Special considerations are also provided for plaid and most striped fabrics. Review the next steps before proceeding.

Identifying the Grainlines

The grainline is drawn on each pattern piece to indicate the direction in which the pattern should be placed on the fabric.

The grainline of the pattern is placed parallel to the selvedges of the fabric. Another popular grainline that is often marked on commercial patterns is the fold line. This is also the lengthwise grain of the fabric.

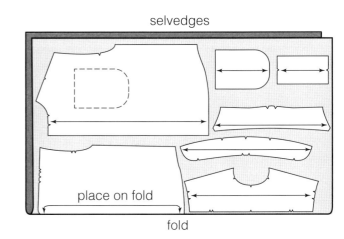

Two-way Directional Pattern Layout

The top and bottom of the pattern pieces may be placed in two different directions (but still following the grain of the fabric) when using a solid or multidirectional print fabric. If you are not sure whether a print is multidirectional, ask the salesperson at the fabric shop.

One-way Directional Pattern Layout

This pattern layout is for one-way designs, such as nap, pile, knitted, striped or plain fabrics. In a one-way directional layout, all pattern pieces are placed facing in the same direction. In other words, the top of each pattern piece will be placed to the right, and the hems will be placed to the left. Be sure to use a one-way directional layout for knitted fabrics and fabric that has a one-way design, stripe or plaid. This will ensure that all stripes and plaids will match, all fabric shading will be in the same direction (for nap or pile fabrics), and all design features will be in the same direction.

STUDIO TIPS

- Always plan the layout on the wrong side of the folded fabric with correct sides together. This makes markings easy to transfer and protects the fabric from damage as it is being handled. Fold the fabric on the lengthwise grain and align the selvedges.

- For many fabrics, the correct side is obvious because of the nap or print. However, the correct side of the fabric might be difficult to determine. In this case, fold back one corner and compare the two surfaces. The correct side might have a brighter print or a shinier surface than the wrong side. If you can't determine which is intended to be the correct side, select the side you like the best and be sure to use the same side throughout the project. Mark the wrong side with chalk to help identify the layers.

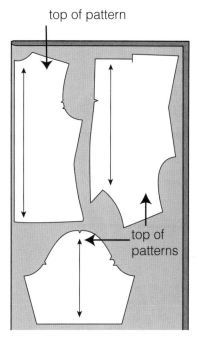

top of pattern

top of patterns

two-way directional layout

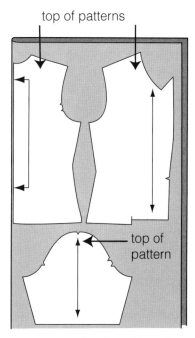

top of patterns

top of pattern

one-way directional layout

- When laying out nap or pile fabric, place the fabric correct side to correct side by gently smoothing and placing the layers on top of each other. Do not smooth out the surface using the palm of your hand because this stretches the fabric and locks the nap threads to each other; they will unlock and unstretch after cutting.

Striped or Plaid Fabric

PREPARING STRIPED FABRICS

When laying out striped fabric on the cutting table, make sure all stripes match on both layers of the fabric.

PREPARING PLAID FABRICS

Plaid fabric must be laid out so that all lengthwise and crosswise stripes of the plaid match on both layers of the fabric. Lay a piece of paper (such as newsprint paper) on the table first. Then, lay the fabric over the paper and pin all the selvedges of the fabric to one side of the paper. Next, fold the fabric on top of the first layer (selvedge to selvedge), pinning and matching all stripes (or plaid stripes) on both layers. If the stripes do not match automatically, the fabric might need to be blocked (see Blocking on page 64).

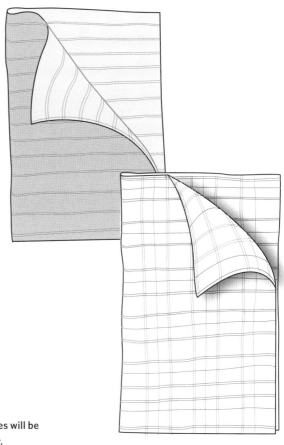

STUDIO TIP When matching lengthwise stripes, the selvedges will be parallel, but not necessarily on top of each other.

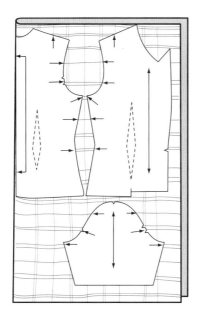

PATTERN LAYOUT FOR STRIPED OR PLAID FABRICS

First work with the pattern pieces that require placement on the fabric fold (this varies from style to style). Note and transfer the location of the stripes (both lengthwise and crosswise) from the fabric to the pattern piece. Mark the pattern pieces with pencil at the shoulder, side seam and armhole notches. Transfer the same stripe markings to the pattern pieces that are sewn to the seam of the first pattern piece. These markings will help match shoulder seams to shoulder seams, side seams to side seams, and so on. The sleeve cap notches will match to the armhole notches. Place these marked pattern pieces on the fabric, making sure all stripes of the fabric (lengthwise and crosswise) match the marks on the pattern pieces.

Pattern Layout for Interfacing

Lay the pattern pieces that need to be interfaced on to the interfacing fabric. Place all pattern pieces following the lengthwise grain of the pattern to the lengthwise grain of the fabric. Place the pattern pieces that need two layers on a double layer of interfacing; place pattern pieces that need one layer of interfacing on a single layer of the interfacing. Pin pattern pieces in place.

selvedges

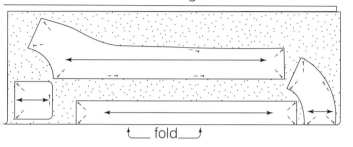

fold

Pattern Layout for Lining

The layout of the lining pattern pieces also follows the lengthwise grain of the fabric. Place the pattern on a double layer of the lining fabric, on the fold if necessary. Pin pattern pieces in place.

STUDIO TIP

BLOCK FUSING INTERFACING is the process of selecting all pattern pieces requiring interfacing. Calculate the amount of fabric the interfacing pieces will require. Precut this amount from the fashion fabric. Using the same amount of interfacing, steam and press the interfacing to the wrong side of the fashion fabric. Cut the fabric and the interfacing at the same time. The pieces will not distort.

Pinning the Pattern to the Fabric

After all pattern pieces have been pinned to the grainline or the fold, finish the pinning process. Keeping the pins well inside the cutting lines, place a pin at each pattern corner and every few centimetres. Be careful not to overpin the pattern, because this will distort the fabric. Keep the pattern flat as you pin. Place pieces as close together as possible. Complete the pattern layout.

GRAINLINES AND FOLDLINES

1 Start with the pattern pieces that are to be placed on the fold. Pin the pattern fold line exactly on the fabric fold. These pattern pieces should be pinned before all other pieces.

2 Pin one end of the grainline to the straight grain of the fabric. Move the pattern piece until the other end of the grainline measures exactly the same distance from the selvedge or fold of the fabric as the first pinned end.

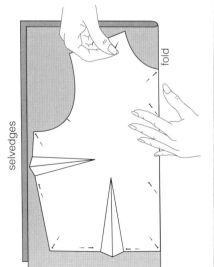

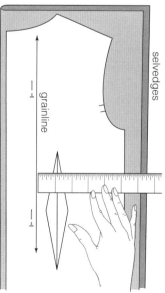

Cutting the Pattern and the Fabric

Keep the fabric flat on the table. Cut with the bulk of the pattern to the left of the scissors (reverse if you are left-handed). Keep one hand on the pattern, close to the cutting line, and manipulate the shears with the other hand.

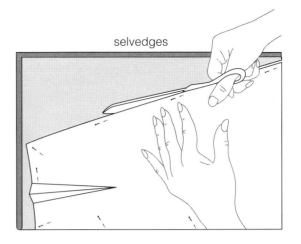

selvedges

STUDIO TIP

Use the whole blade and close the scissors to the tips – do not make short, chopping movements.

TRANSFERRING PATTERN MARKINGS

Correctly transferring the pattern markings from the pattern to the fabric is very important for sewing all the design details accurately. Markings include notches, darts, tucks, pleats, fold lines, centre front positions, centre back positions and pocket placements.

Quick and Easy Pattern Marking Method

1 Snip notches, darts, tucks, pleats, fold lines, and centre front and centre back positions with the point of the scissors.

2 Place an awl or a pin through the pattern and both layers of the fabric 13mm before the end of the dart tip.

3 With a pencil or an awl, mark this position of the dart on the fabric.

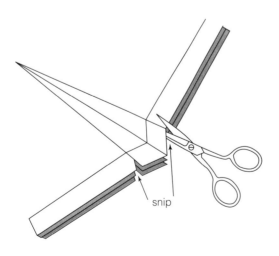

snip

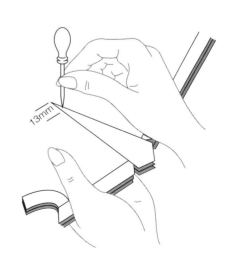

13mm

Pencil Marking Method

1 Insert a pin at each dart point, at each button and pocket placement and for other pattern symbols that cannot be snipped.

2 On the wrong side of the fabric, using a pencil or chalk, mark the position of the pin with a dot.

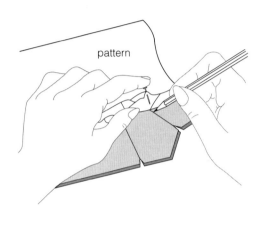

pattern

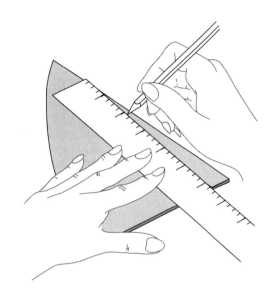

Tracing Wheel Marking Method

Place dressmaker's carbon paper on the wrong side of the fabric and use a tracing wheel to trace pattern markings.

Bear in mind, however, that the tracing wheel method might not be accurate. As the pattern is lifted to insert the tracing paper, the fabric and/or pattern might slip out of position. Also, the marks left by the tracing wheel can sometimes show through the fabric.

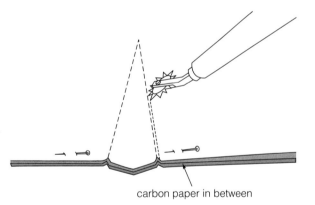

carbon paper in between

CHAPTER

5

STITCHES

- Key Terms and Concepts

- Crimping and Ease Stitching

- Gathering

- Stretching and Sewing Elastic

- Hemming Stitches

KEY TERMS *and* CONCEPTS

Sewing stitches are created in a complete sewing action, using a threaded needle. They can be produced either by hand or machine. Stitches may be functional or decorative, and they may be concealed within or show on the face of a garment.

Permanent stitches are used for seams, darts and tucks. The length and tension of the stitch vary, depending on the fabric used. On most medium-weight fabrics, there are about ten to 12 stitches per inch; sheers require a finer stitch length, about 14 stitches per inch; heavyweight fabric is usually sewn at eight to ten stitches per inch.

Regular stitch is a straight, consistent, even-length stitch used as a permanent stitch.

Basting stitches are long temporary stitches made by hand or machine, approximately six stitches per inch. Ends are not fastened or backstitched. Before basting stitches are removed, threads are snipped every few inches to facilitate removal.

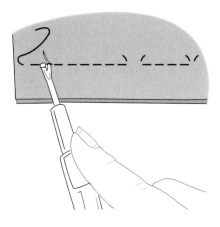

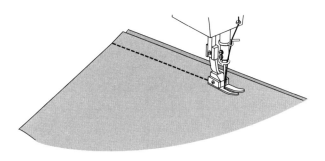

Pin basting is used when pins hold fabric pieces together, so that they can be easily removed as stitched. Use as many pins as necessary to keep the layers of fabric from slipping.

STUDIO TIPS

- **Place a piece of** tissue paper under fabrics such as sheers or smooth, slippery fabrics **to prevent slipping. After stitching, tear the tissue away.**
- When sewing velvet or pile fabrics, **hand baste along the seam line to prevent the fabric from slipping. Stitch the seam in the direction of the pile.**
- Areas where there is strain or a need for reinforcement, **such as points of collars, cuffs and pointed faced openings of necklines, need a finer, tighter stitch, usually 16 to 18 stitches per inch.**

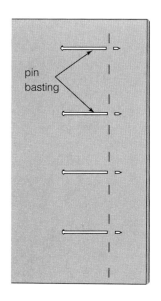

pin basting

Stay stitching is plain machine stitching 3mm inside on the stitchline before the garment is assembled. It is used to maintain the original shape of the garment pieces and to prevent stretching, which is especially necessary in necklines.

Place your index finger behind the foot as you sew to prevent the seam from stretching out the original shape of the fabric.

STUDIO TIP

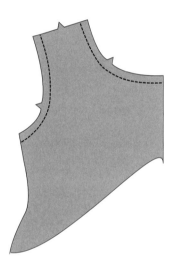

Topstitching is a single row or multiple rows of machine stitching made on the outside of the garment, through all layers of the garment. Topstitching is used to outline seams; attach pockets, plackets or yokes and to add stability to a garment. It is mainly used as a decorative stitch. Most topstitching is placed 6mm from the edge.

Topstitching is usually made with a longer-than-usual straight stitch. The stitch length should be set to six to eight stitches per inch.

Topstitching is a smart and practical way to accent the seams of a fashion garment. Although matching thread is usually used, a decorative effect can be obtained by using a contrasting thread or buttonhole twist as the upper thread. Because topstitching is visible on a garment, it requires careful placement and execution.

When positioning topstitching, always follow a guide. The edge of the presser foot is the most common guide used to apply straight and accurate topstitching. Other guides include a strip of masking tape, lines marked on the machine, and a guide attached to the throat plate or presser foot of the machine, such as a quilting guide.

Zigzag stitches are machine stitches that have a saw-toothed shape. Zigzag stitches are used to join two pieces of fabric together to create a decorative design. The stitch length and width can be varied, depending upon the desired effect. Using a zigzag stitch on the seam edge will prevent fraying. Zigzag stitches can also be used when sewing knit.

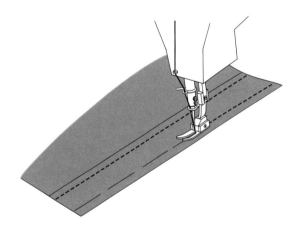

Edge stitching is stitching that is close to the seamline. Edge stitching should be within 1.5mm of the edge; if it is more than 1.5mm from the edge, it is considered to be topstitching.

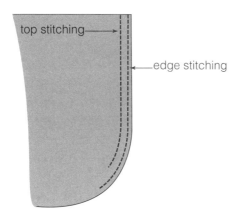

top stitching
edge stitching

Understitching is a row of stitching on the facing or under layer that keeps the facing, under layer or seam edge from rolling to the outside of the garment.

When understitching, press the facing away from the garment and position all the layers of the seam allowance to the facing side. On the correct side of the facing, machine stitch close to the seam edge. While stitching, gently pull the facing and the garment sections on both sides of the stitchline to help make both pieces lay flat.

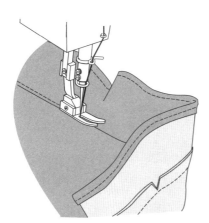

Stitching in the ditch is sewing in the ridge of a previously stitched seam, on the correct side of the garment. Because it is sewn into the ridge of a seam, it is an inconspicuous stitch. It is used to complete waistbands, cuffs, collars and French bias binding, when visible stitching is not desired. Use regular stitch length and match the thread to the fabric.

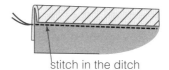

stitch in the ditch

Directional stitching prevents seam stretching. In general, shoulder seams are stitched from the neckline to the armhole; side seams from the underarm to the waistline; sleeve seams from the underarm to the wrist; and skirt/trouser seams from the hem to the waistline.

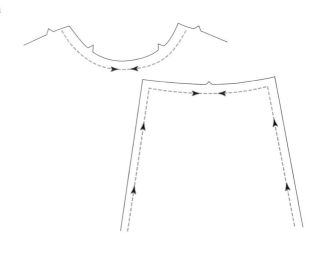

CRIMPING *and* EASE STITCHING

Crimping and **ease stitching** are stitching methods used when one edge of a garment is slightly longer than the matching edge that is to be sewn to it. In order for the seam to appear smooth and not pucker or pleat, the longer piece must be crimped, or ease-stitched, to the shorter piece.

Crimping and ease stitching are most commonly used on sleeve caps, neckline edges that have been stretched out, princess seam curves over the bustline, and turned hems on slightly flared skirts.

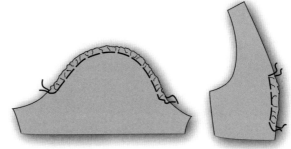

Crimping

1 Place the left index finger tightly behind the presser foot and machine stitch a single row of stitching on the stitchline. Allow the fabric to flow freely under the presser foot and machine stitch a single row of crimping on the stitchline. Fabric will pile up between the index finger and the presser foot. This puckers and crimps in the fabric.

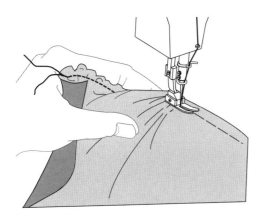

2 Distribute the crimping evenly. Placing the right sides of the fabric together, pin the shorter seam to the crimped seam, placing a pin approximately every 13mm.

3 Keeping the crimped seam on top, stitch along the stitchline. Sew the two seams to each other, using a regular machine stitch. Be careful not to sew in any folds or gathers.

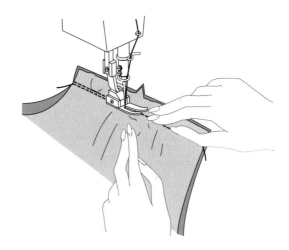

Ease Stitching

Machine stitch a double row of basting stitches close to the seamline and pull the threads to the desired fullness (it should be a minimal amount of fullness). Refer to Using a Basting Stitch on pages 98–99.)

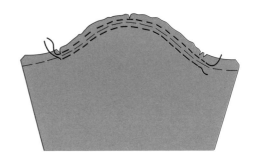

GATHERING

Gathering is the process of drawing up fabric fullness along the stitchline and distributing the fullness where desired. Many garments require that pieces be gathered before they are sewn into a seam. Gathers may be used in a garment section or design detail, such as ruffles, ruchings and flounces; dirndl skirts; full or puffed sleeves; and style lines on a dress or blouse.

Gathering Foot

Most sewing machines include a gathering foot, which will automatically sew a single row or multiple rows of gathers quickly and evenly. Because the foot is designed to lock fullness into every stitch, it ensures evenly spaced gathers. The shape of this foot varies from machine to machine, but it usually has a 'hump' on the bottom.

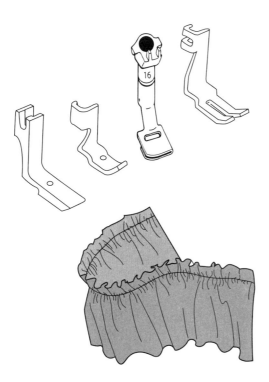

1 To gather, place your left index finger tightly behind the **gathering foot**, and machine stitch a single row of gathers on the stitchline, from the beginning to the end of the area that needs to be gathered. Allow the fabric to flow freely under the gathering foot. Fabric will pile up between your index finger and the presser foot. Lift your finger to release some fabric. Replace your finger near the back of the gathering foot and repeat until the entire area is gathered.

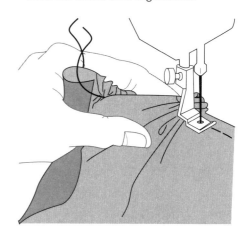

STUDIO TIP

The stitch length on the sewing machine controls the amount of fullness. A longer stitch length creates more fullness and a shorter stitch length creates less fullness. For maximum fullness on heavier fabrics, it might be necessary to tighten the tension.

2 Distribute the gathers evenly. Place correct sides of the fabric together and pin the shorter seam to the gathered seam. Place the gathered garment section on top. Pin approximately every 13mm.

3 Keeping the gathered section on top, stitch along the stitchline. Sew the two pieces to each other, using a regular machine stitch. Be careful not to catch any folds.

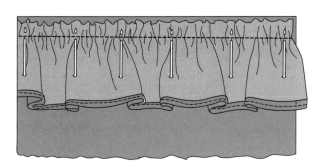

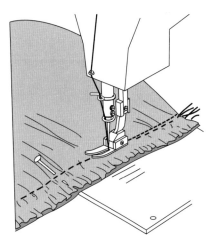

GATHERING VARIATION: Another way of making gathers is to sew a double row of basting stitches and pull the bobbin threads until you achieve the desired fullness.

STRETCHING *and* SEWING ELASTIC

Elastic is often used to gather a ruffle or the bottom of a sleeve, or to introduce fullness to a fitting area in a garment (such as the waist seam).

1 Distribute the elastic in half (and in quarters, if needed) and mark with a pin. Divide the garment area requiring the elastic, and mark with a pin.

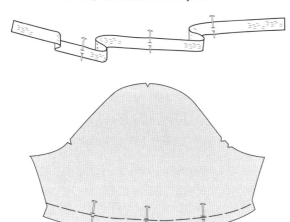

2 Place the elastic on top of the wrong side of the garment, noting divided positions. Starting from the edge of the garment, tack the end of the elastic to the edge of the garment area requiring the elastic.

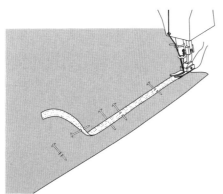

3 With the machine needle in the down position, stretch the first portion of the elastic to the first divided position. Stitch the elastic to the garment until the first divided position is reached. Repeat this stretching and sewing technique until the elastic is completely attached.

NOTE: The garment will look gathered; however, it will stretch when needed when the garment is being put on.

NOTE: A zigzag stitch may also be used with regular thread in both the needle and the bobbin.

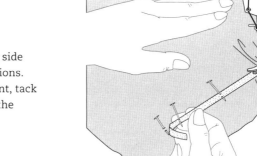

STUDIO TIP

Use elastic thread in the bobbin to give gathered effects in garment pieces. Wind elastic thread on the bobbin by hand. Be sure not to stretch the elastic. Use regular thread as the upper thread.

HEMMING STITCHES

Several stitches can be used to hem a garment. Select thread to match the garment. Fullness should be eased in and distributed evenly for a flat, smooth finish.

Hem stitches should be spaced evenly and inconspicuously sewn to the fabric. Select one of the following stitches as appropriate for the garment and fabric.

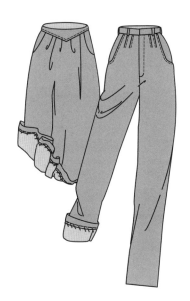

Pick Stitch

A **pick stitch** is a small, durable backstitch used to hand finish a hem or a zipper application. It is also called hand pick stitch.

1   Pick up a small stitch of the garment with the needle.

2   About 6mm from the hem edge, pick up another stitch.

3   Continue to stitch, taking a stitch first in the garment and then in the hem edge, until the hem is finished.

Catch Stitch

A **catch stitch** is a hand-worked, short backstitch, taken alternately from left to right, ply to ply, to form a close cross stitch. It is used especially for hemming.

1   Take a small, horizontal stitch in the garment, from right to left, near the edge of the hem.

2   Pick up a thread of the garment diagonally, below and to the right of the first stitch.

3   Continue to stitch in this zigzag pattern until the hem is finished.

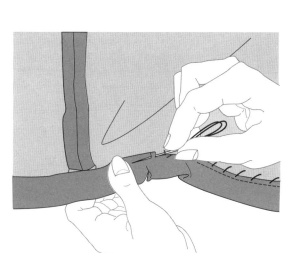

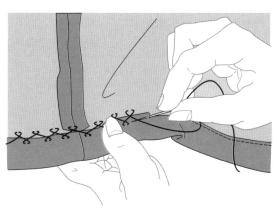

Slipstitch or Blindstitch

A **slipstitch** or **blindstitch** is an almost invisible small hand stitch used for hemming. The thread is concealed by slipping the needle through a fold in the fabric with each stitch.

1 Pick up a small, inconspicuous stitch of the garment with the needle.

2 Take another small stitch in the hem edge, diagonally.

3 Continue to stitch, taking a small stitch first in the garment and then in the hem edge, until the hem is finished.

blindstitch

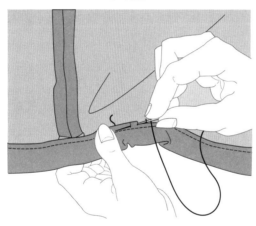

slipstitch

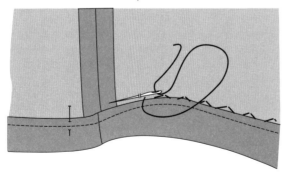

Narrow Stitch Hem

A **narrow stitch hem** is a machine-stitched narrow hem used on the bottom of shirts, blouses, and some skirts.

1 Fold the garment edge under 6mm and fold the hem allowance (usually 13mm) up along the stitching line.

2 Edge stitch the folded edge in place by machine.

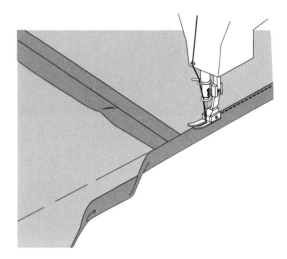

Rolled Hem or Merrow Hem

A **rolled hem** or **merrow hem** is a distinctive stitch; an overlocker is used to clean-finish a hem or raw edge of scarves, skirts, napkins and dresses to give the appearance of a satin finish. Domestic overlockers require a special setting, whereas a special overlock produces the merrow edge in the fashion industry. No additional turning or stitch is required for this hem.

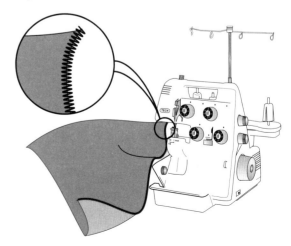

CHAPTER
6

SEAMS *and*
SHAPING

- Seams

- Seam Finishes

- Darts

- Sewing Darts

- Pleats

- Tucks

SEAMS

Seams are created in the process of matching and sewing two or more pieces of fabric together to form a finished edge. The type of seam selected should be appropriate for the fabric, type of garment and location of the seam in the garment.

Seams are stitched in the following direction:
- Shoulder seams – from the neckline to the armhole.
- Bodice side seams – from the underarm to the waistline or hem.
- Sleeve seams – from the underarm to the wrist.
- Skirt seams – from the hem to the waistline.

The **seam allowance** is the excess fabric needed to sew a seam, varying from 6–25mm. The standard amount for domestic sewing is 16mm.

Backstitch is the reverse stitch on the machine. You backstitch by sewing back and forth to reinforce the stitching at the beginning and end of a seam.

The **stitchline** is the sewing/stitching line on a pattern.

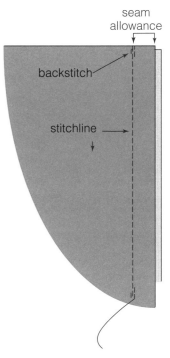

The **stitch length in a seam** depends on the type of stitch needed for that specific garment area:
- A **permanent machine-stitched seam** is sewn at ten to 12 stitches per inch. Ends are not backstitched, so the seam can be removed easily.
- A **reinforced stitch in a seam** uses very short stitches, 16 to 18 stitches per inch, and reinforces an area subject to strain, such as corners.

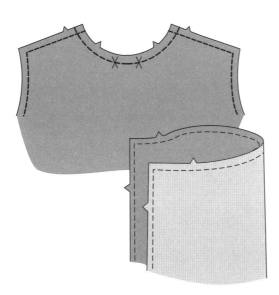

10   12   14

The **seam guidelines** assist in guiding the stitching straight and parallel to the seam edge. Seam guidelines are usually marked on the throat plate of the sewing machine. The lines, which are usually numbered in 3mm increments, indicate the width of the seam allowance desired for the garment pieces.

The **presser foot** is the attachment on the sewing machine that holds fabric steady at the point where it is being advanced, while the needle is stitching. The all-purpose foot is used for most stitching.

Sewing Guidelines

Always start and finish stitching with the needle and foot in the up position. There should be 12.7cm of the thread behind the presser foot.

Place the fabric under the presser foot with the cut edges to the right of the needle and lined up with the seam allowance guideline on the throat plate. This should position the seamline directly under the needle.

Lower the presser foot and lightly hold the fabric as it passes under the needle. At the same time, guide the fabric parallel to the seam guidelines on the throat plate. Look at the cut edge of the garment – not at the needle – as the fabric moves through the sewing machine. Stitch forward 6mm and then back to the edge of the fabric and forwards again along the stitchline to complete the plain seam. At the end of the stitchline, backstitch 6mm and then stitch forward to the edge of the fabric.

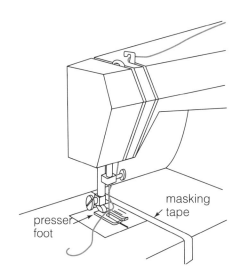

presser foot

masking tape

STUDIO TIP

Place a strip of masking tape along the chosen seam guideline on the throat plate to provide a seam guideline all the way across the sewing area of the machine.

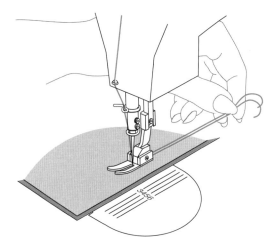

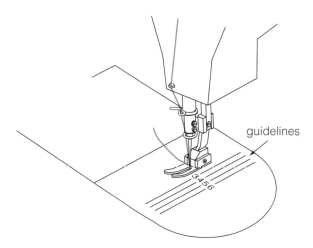

guidelines

Plain Seam

The **plain seam** is the most common seam used to sew two garment pieces together. It is used on side seams, shoulder seams and style lines. The plain seam is used on most fabrics, except knits. The stitch length is between ten and 12 stitches per inch for most fabrics. The width of the seam allowance is usually 16mm for fashion sewing and 13mm for industry sewing.

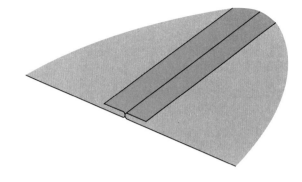

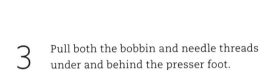

1   Place one piece of fabric on the sewing table, with the correct side up.

3   Pull both the bobbin and needle threads under and behind the presser foot.

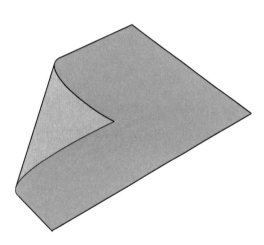

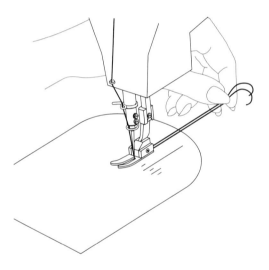

2   Place the second piece of fabric on the first piece, with correct sides together.

4   Place both pieces of fabric under the presser foot at the beginning of the garment piece stitchline, with the edge of the fabric on the seam guidelines on the sewing machine throat plate.

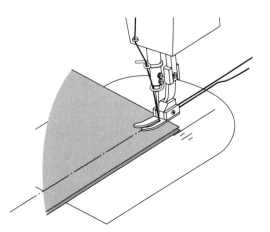

5 Stitch forward 6mm then back to edge of fabric, then forwards again along the stitchline to complete the plain seam. Follow the seam guidelines on the sewing machine throat plate.

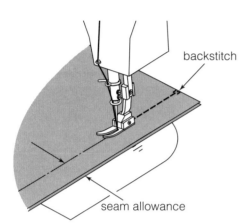

backstitch

seam allowance

7 Pull the fabric and the attached threads behind the presser foot and clip the threads close to the fabric.

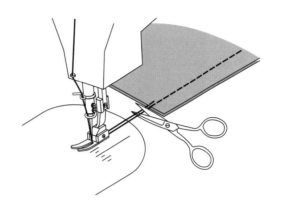

6 At the end of the stitchline, backstitch 6mm and then stitch forward to edge of fabric.

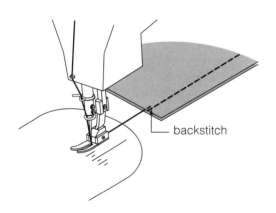

backstitch

8 Press the seam open.

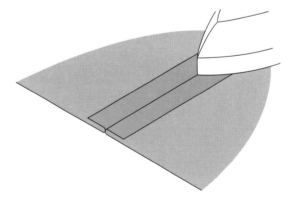

Using a Basting Stitch

A **basting stitch** is used to sew two pieces of fabric together when a temporary seam is needed. This may be in the slot seam, an open welt seam or the preliminary seam for setting a railroad zip. It may also be used in seam areas of the garment for preliminary fittings. The stitch length is about 6 stitches per inch and is generally the longest stitch on the machine. The width of the seam allowance is the same as that of the plain seam.

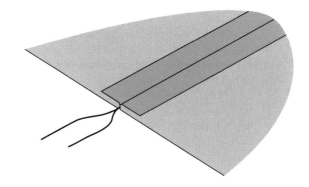

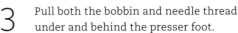

1 Place one piece of fabric on the sewing table, with the correct side up.

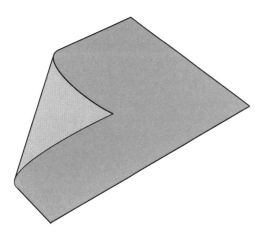

2 Place the second piece of fabric on the first piece, with the correct sides together.

3 Pull both the bobbin and needle threads under and behind the presser foot.

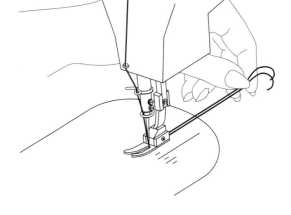

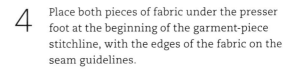

4 Place both pieces of fabric under the presser foot at the beginning of the garment-piece stitchline, with the edges of the fabric on the seam guidelines.

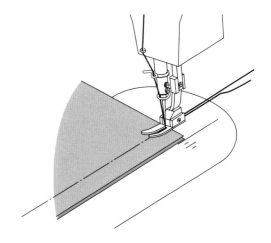

5 Following the seam guidelines, use the longest stitch. Do not backstitch. Continue sewing along the stitchline to complete the seam.

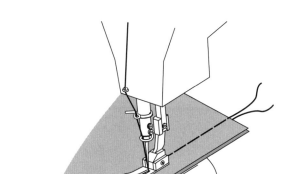

7 Press the seam open.

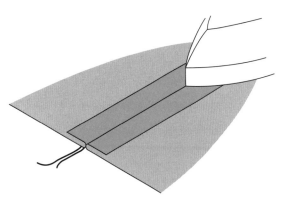

6 Pull the fabric and the attached threads behind the presser foot, and clip the threads halfway between the fabric and the needle.

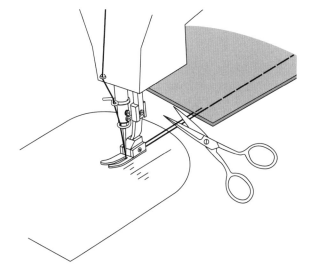

Slot Seam

A **slot seam** is desirable when a strip of lace fabric or a matching or contrasting strip of fabric is added to the underlay area of the seam. After the basting stitch is removed from the stitched seam, the backing strip shows between the finished seam edges. This seam can also add a bit of spice to an otherwise plain seam, used mostly in yoke seams.

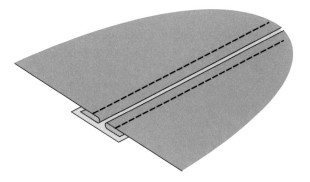

1   Sew a plain seam using a basting stitch. Refer to Using a Basting Stitch on pages 98–99.

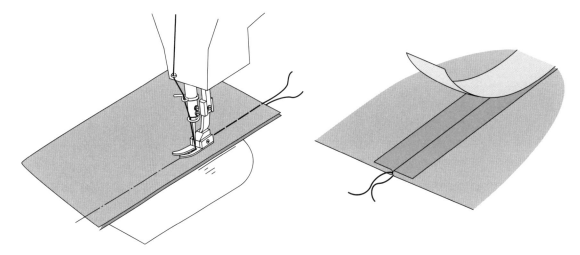

3   Cut a strip of matching or contrasting fabric the same width as the two seam edges. Lay the strip in place as illustrated. Pin if necessary.

2   Press the seam open.

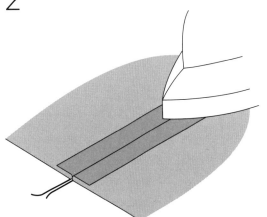

4   Turn the garment over, with the correct side of the fabric up and the strip still in position.

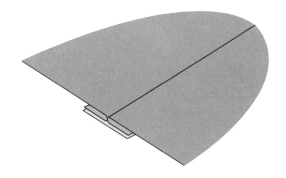

5 Using the presser foot as a guide, stitch 6mm away from the seamline with a straight machine stitch.

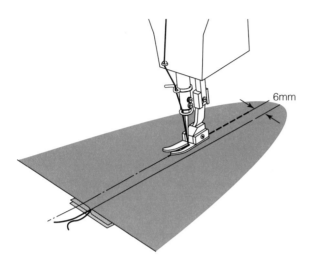

7 Remove the basting stitches.

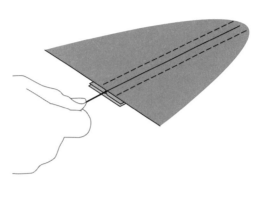

6 Repeat on the opposite seamline and press in place.

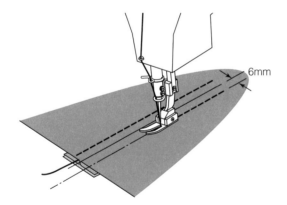

French Seam

The **French seam** is a narrow seam within a seam, which encloses the raw edges of fabric so that fraying does not occur. This seam is used on sheer fabrics and lingerie to conceal the raw edges. This seam gives a finished seam look from the outside of the garment, as well as from the inside. It is not recommended for curved seams because they tend to buckle.

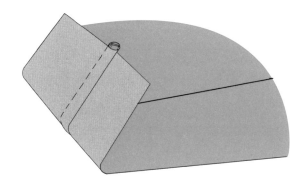

1 Place the garment pieces on the sewing table, with the wrong sides together. Follow the seam guidelines on the throat plate, and stitch with a 6mm seam allowance. Backstitch as illustrated for a plain seam (see page 97).

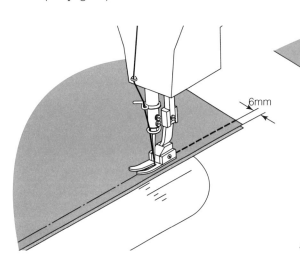

6mm

2 Trim the seam allowance to 3mm.

3mm

3 Press the seam allowance open.

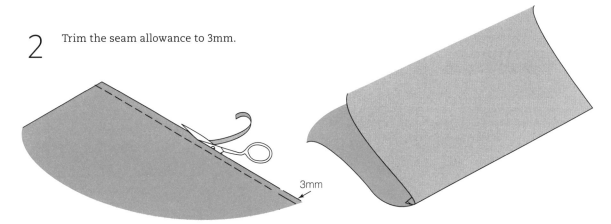

4 Fold the fabric so that the correct sides are together.

5   Stitch a new 6mm seam allowance. Backstitch as illustrated for a plain seam (see page 97).

6   Turn the garment over, to the correct side. Press the seam flat to one side. Notice that the seam is now enclosed, which gives a finished seam look from the outside of the garment and an enclosed seam on the inside of the garment.

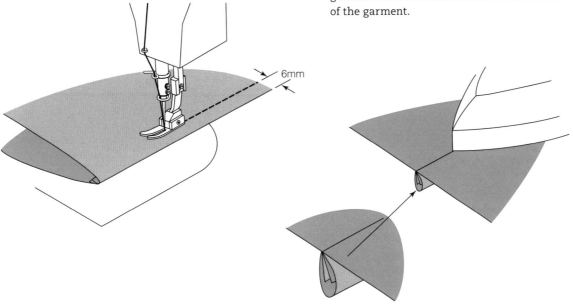

6mm

STUDIO TIP

The enclosed French seam may be placed on the outside of the garment for a decorative or 'edgy' look.

Flat-felled Seam

The **flat-felled seam** provides a clean finish to both sides of the garment. Two rows of stitching show on the outside of the seam. This type of seam is usually used to give strong, non-fraying, durable construction for sportswear and reversible garments.

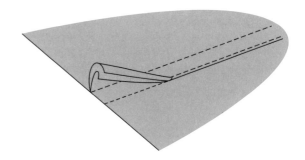

1 Place the garment pieces on the sewing table, with wrong sides together.

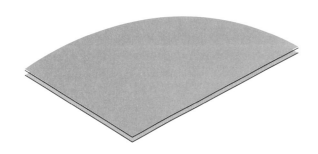

2 Sew a plain seam (refer to Plain Seam on pages 96–97). Press to one side.

3 Fold over both edges of the seam 6mm.

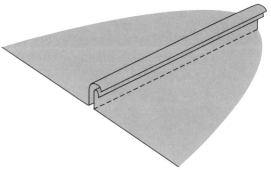

4 Lay seam allowance flat, as illustrated.

5 Using the needle as the sewing guide, stitch the edge of the fold through all the layers of fabric.

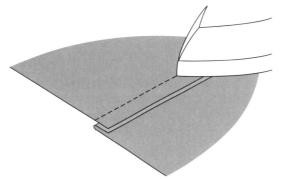

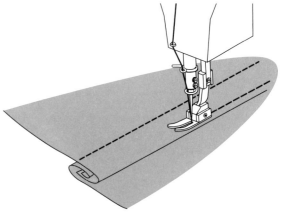

Corded Seam

The **corded seam** is a decorative seam or edge and can be used as a design feature on garments or home fashion accessories, such as cushions. Corded seams are used in necklines, collar edges and pocket edges to accentuate the outer edges of these pieces. A corded seam gives a stiff finish and should be used in medium-weight fabrics.

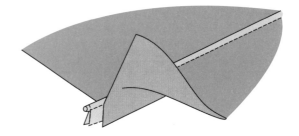

1 With a piece of fabric correct side up, place the raw edge of the cording even with edge of fabric. Baste stitch the cording to the seam allowance along the stitching line.

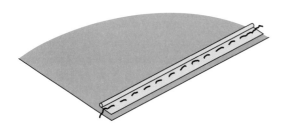

2 Place the second piece of fabric, with the correct side down, over the cording. Make sure all the edges are even.

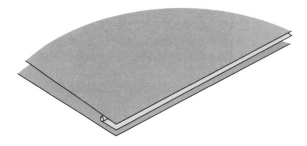

3 Using a cording foot or a zipper foot, stitch along the edge of the cording on the seamline.

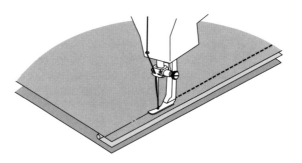

STUDIO TIP

For an outside curved seam with cording, stretch the seam allowance around the outside curve and ease the cording. For an inside curved seam with cording, stretch the cord and slightly ease in the seam allowance.

Curved Seam

A **curved seam** is used to provide shaping, usually in a style line of a garment, such as on a princess seam, bodice yoke or skirt yoke.

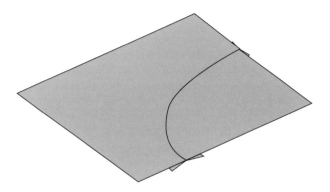

1   Place a garment piece with a concave curve on the sewing table, with the correct side up.

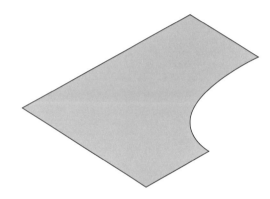

3   Start stitching in the same way as for a plain seam (pages 96–97).

4   Continue sewing to the point where the stitchline (or the edges of the fabric) begin to diverge.

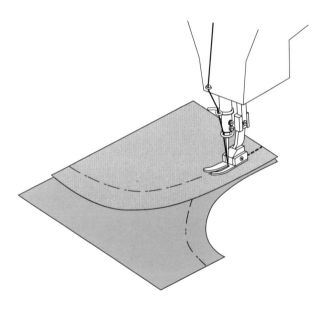

2   Place a garment piece with a convex curve on the first piece, with the wrong side up, as illustrated.

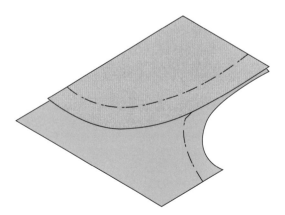

5   Turn the needle down into the fabric and raise the presser foot.

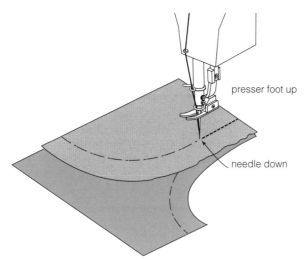

presser foot up

needle down

6   Pivot the top fabric around the needle until the stitchline or fabric edges converge.

7   Continue stitching.

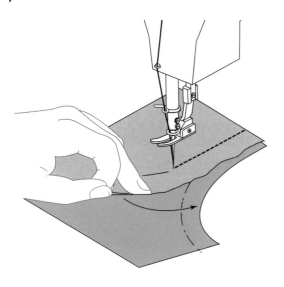

8   Repeat this procedure until the seam is completed.

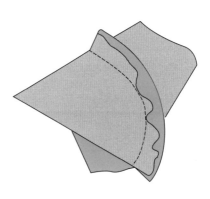

9   Press the entire seam to one side.

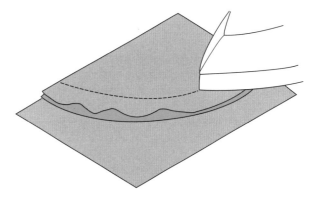

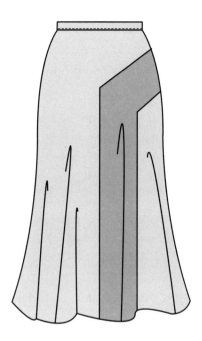

Corner or Pointed Seam

A **corner or pointed seam** is a seam featured in a square yoke, a square or V-shape style line or neckline. The sewing method used to turn the corner of these areas is a bit tricky because the corner must be pivoted exactly on the stitchline of the corner or V shape. The sewing method used to turn a corner can be applied to other angular seams, such as those in godets or pointed yokes.

1 Place the first garment piece of fabric (usually the larger piece) on the sewing table, with the correct side up.

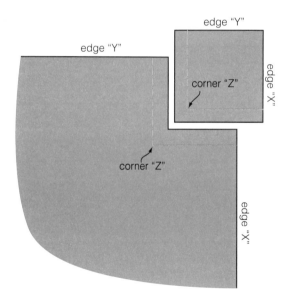

NOTE: For this activity, label the callouts for the edges X and Y and the corner of the stitchline Z.

2 Place the second garment piece on top of the first piece, with the correct sides together, matching stitchlines (in this example, matching Y edges and stitchlines).

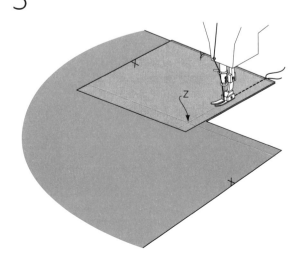

3 Stitch, on the stitchline, to the corner Z.

4 With the needle down, lift the presser foot up. Keep your garment on the machine with the needle holding it in place at corner Z.

6 With the needle down and the presser foot up, pivot the top layer of fabric on the needle at the stitchline corner Z. Continue pivoting the top layer until it meets the stitchline on the bottom layer (in this example, matching X edges and stitchlines).

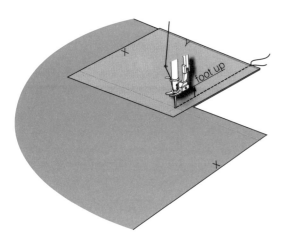

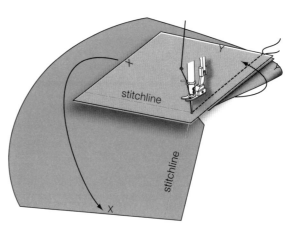

5 Carefully clip the bottom layer of fabric into the corner Z (be sure not to clip the stitching by stopping 1.5mm from the corner).

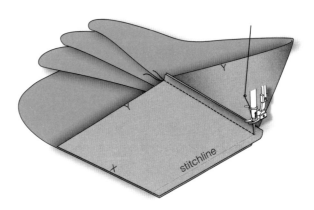

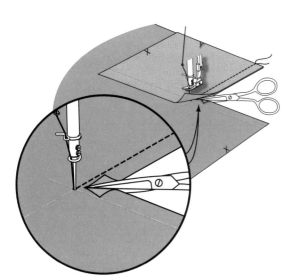

7 Continue to sew on the stitchline until the seam is completed.

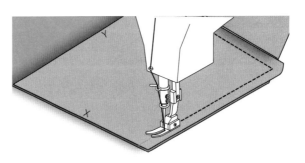

Shirt Yoke Seam

The traditional **shirt yoke seam** can be designed with a variety of yoke styles and centre-front plackets, either as a dress shirt or sport shirt for women, men and children. The yoke is usually fully lined with the same fabric as the garment. However, on a quilted flannel shirt, the yoke is usually lined with lining fabric.

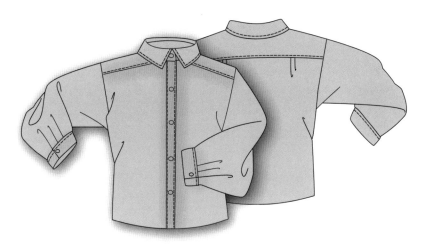

1   Sew all tucks and pleats. Notice the pleats in the back shirt piece (sometimes there is only one, at the centre back).

2   Sew the outside yoke piece and the lining yoke piece to the back shirt piece, sandwiching the shirt piece between the yokes.

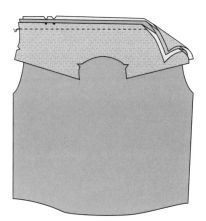

3 Match the right and left front
shirt pieces to the yoke lining
(one layer only).

NOTE: The correct side of the yoke
lining will match to the wrong side of
the front shirt pieces, that is, correct
side to wrong side.

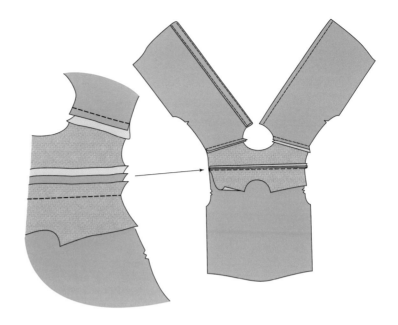

4 Press the yoke pieces up and topstitch this
back yoke seam.

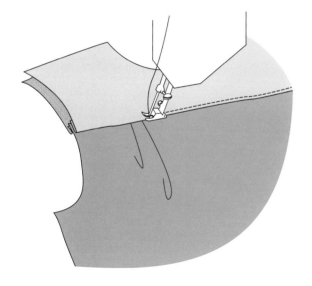

5 Press the yoke seams toward the yoke. Press
the seam allowance of the top yoke and pin
baste the yoke over the stitchline of the front
yoke seam. Edge stitch the top layer of the
yoke to the garment.

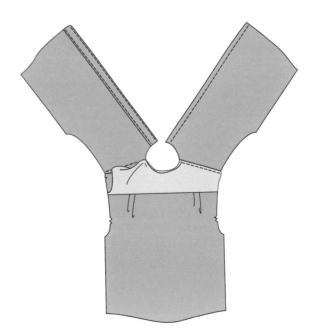

Ruffle Applied in a Seam

This **ruffled technique** illustrates how to sew
a purchased gathered decorative trim or a prepared
gathered piece into the style edge of a collar, cuff
or blouse facing.

1 Pin the prepared or purchased ruffle to the
outer edge of the garment piece. The wrong
side of the ruffle should be placed facing the
correct side of the garment edge.

2 Baste the ruffled edge in place.

3 Place and pin baste the facing layer on top
of the ruffled layer.

4 Stitch the outer layer seam along the
stitchline, for the entire length of the
outer seam.

5 Turn the garment piece correct side out.
Understitch. Press the outer edge flat.

NOTE: For a 'stand up' ruffle, attach the correct side
of the ruffle to the correct side of the garment.

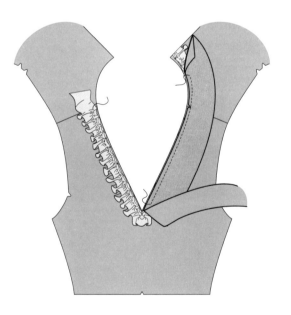

SEAM FINISHES

Plain Seam with a Self, Clean-Edge Finish

The **self, clean-edge seam** is a quick and neat method of finishing a plain seam. This finishing method prevents the cut edges of the seams from unraveling on certain fabrics, such as coarse weaves and tweeds. It also helps to give a more finished look in garments such as unlined jackets.

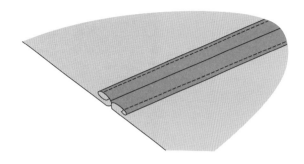

4   Stitch close to the folded edge.

1   Sew a plain seam. Refer to Plain Seam on pages 96–97.

2   Place the garment seam on the sewing table, with the wrong side up and with one seam allowance folded under, as illustrated.

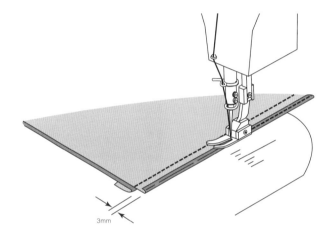

3mm

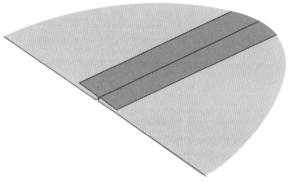

5   Repeat on the other seam allowance.

6   Press the seam open.

3   Fold over the edge of the exposed seam allowance 3mm.

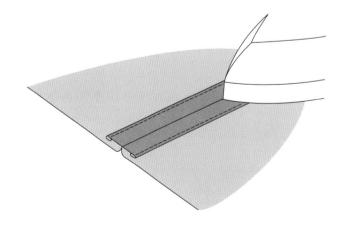

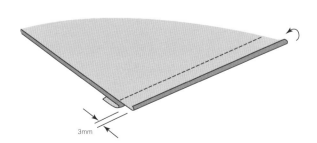

3mm

Plain Seam with Bound Edges

A **bound-edge seam** requires bias tape to finish the raw edges of the seam. This method is desirable when sewing with fabric such as coarse weaves or loosely woven woollens that fray easily. It is also used on fake furs or unlined jackets to give a finished look.

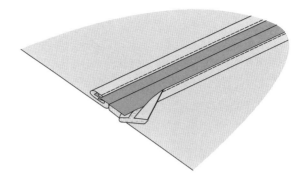

1   Sew a plain seam. Refer to Plain Seam on pages 96–97.

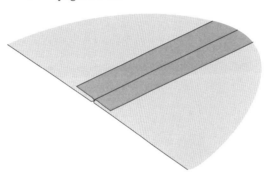

2   Place the garment on the sewing table, with the wrong side of the fabric up, as illustrated.

3   Slip purchased bias over one edge of the seam allowance.

4   Edge stitch along the fold of the bias tape.

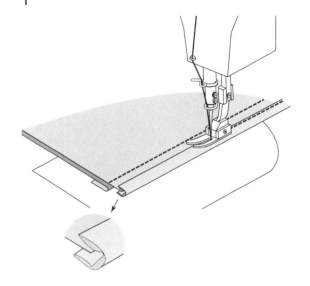

5   Repeat this procedure on the opposite seam allowance and press the seam open.

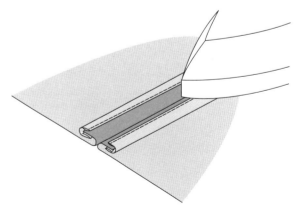

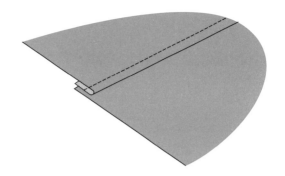

Welt Seam

A **welt seam** allows the plain seam to be 'detailed' with topstitching in matching or contrasting thread. This seam finish is used most often in princess-style seams and yoke seams, often with firm fabrics. This seam provides a strong seam construction and gives a decorative effect.

1   Sew a plain seam. Refer to Plain Seam on pages 96–97.

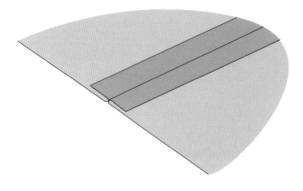

2   Press the seam allowance to one side.

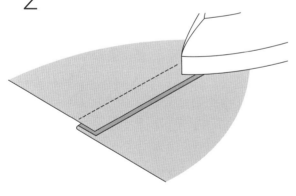

3   Turn both pieces of the fabric over so that the garment is correct side up.

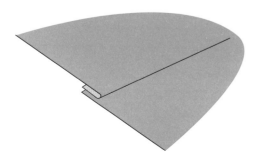

4   Using the presser foot as a guide, stitch 6mm away from the seamline with a straight machine stitch.

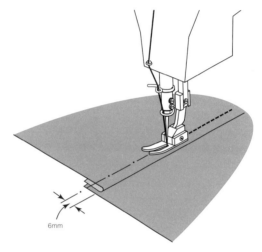

6mm

5   Press in place.

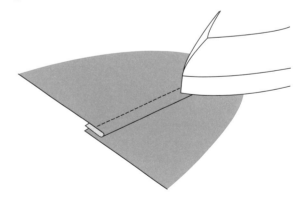

Open Welt Seam

An **open welt seam** is decorative. The seam forms a small tuck and emphasizes a construction detail. This adds interest to a garment and is suitable for almost all fabrics, except sheer fabrics.

1   Sew a plain seam, using a basting stitch. Refer to Using a Basting Stitch on pages 98–99.

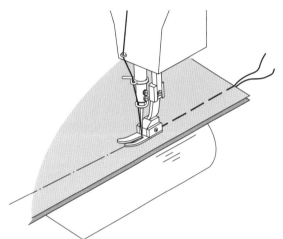

2   Press the seam allowance to one side.

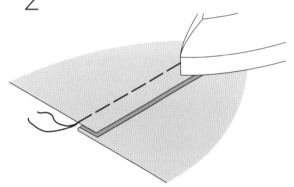

3   Turn both pieces of fabric over so that the correct side faces up.

4   Using the presser foot as a guide, stitch 6mm away from the seamline with a straight machine stitch.

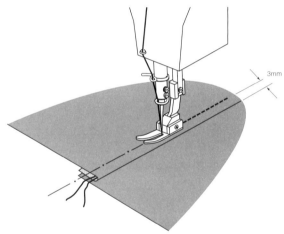

3mm

5   Press in place.

6   Remove the basting stitches.

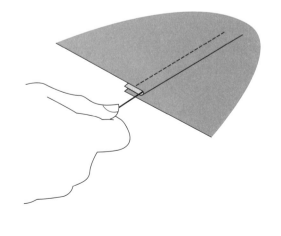

DARTS

A **dart** is the take-up of excess fabric, of various widths, at the edge of a garment converging to a diminishing point. There are several types of darts, as shown in this section. Darts must be positioned and sewn accurately in order to emphasize the lines on the body.

Darts are the most basic structural elements in sewing and are used in:

- The front bodice section, to contour the body.
- The front bodice section, from any perimeter point towards the apex, to shape the fabric over the bust and to contour the body.
- The back bodice waist, to fit fabric to the waistline.
- The back neck or shoulder seam, to shape the fabric over upper shoulder and allow ease over the shoulder blade.
- Fitted sleeves, to allow for elbow movement.
- The front and back sections of skirts and trousers, to shape fabric to the waistline and allow ease over the hips.

Dart legs are the stitchlines on both sides of the dart.

The **dart point** is the vanishing point and the small end of the dart.

The **wide end** of the dart is the widest end of the dart legs.

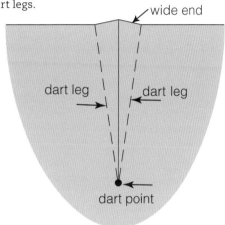

Bust darts help the garment fit over the bust area. They usually begin at the shoulder or side seam and finish 5cm from the bust point (the apex).

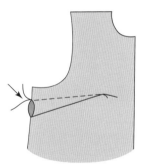

Skirt and trouser darts bring in the waist of a skirt or trousers. The front darts are usually shorter than the back darts.

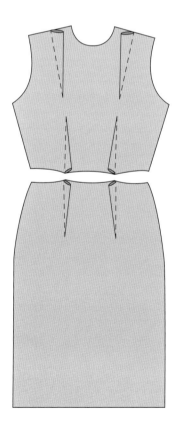

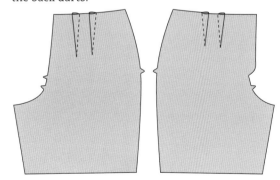

Fisheye darts are most often used on garments without a waistline seam, such as blouses, dresses, waistcoats or jackets, to bring in fullness at the waist. They allow the garment to curve smoothly at the waistline and create ease at hip areas.

The **French dart** is a diagonal dart originating from any point between the hipline to 5cm above the waist, along the side seam and tapering to the apex. This dart could be straight, shaped or cut away, depending on the excess in the dart width.

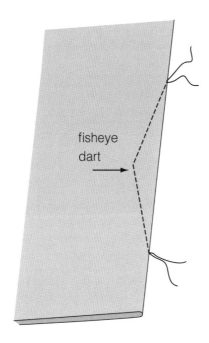

fisheye dart

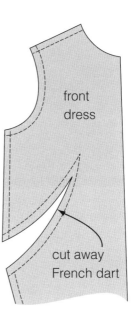

front dress

cut away French dart

SEWING DARTS

Straight Tapered Dart

The straight tapered dart is the basic dart used in a bodice, skirt or sleeve, to give a smooth, rounded fit. This dart creates a rounded fullness at the fullest part of the body.

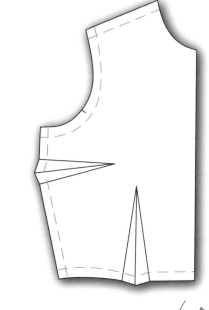

TRANSFERRING STRAIGHT TAPERED DART MARKINGS

Transfer the dart marking from the pattern to the wrong side of the fabric. Refer to Chapter 4 for specific directions.

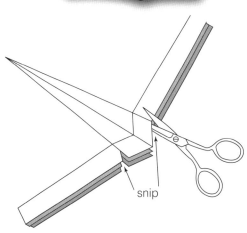

snip

1   With the correct sides of the fabric together, fold the dart so that the snip ends match.

2   Continue to fold the dart (along the centre line) to the punch hole or pencil mark.

3   If necessary, pin and pencil in the stitchline. Refer to Chapter 4 for detailed instructions.

4   Start to sew (and backstitch) from 13mm beyond the punch hole or pencil mark to ensure that the hole is caught. Make sure the needle enters the fabric exactly on the fold at the stitchline for a couple of stitches.

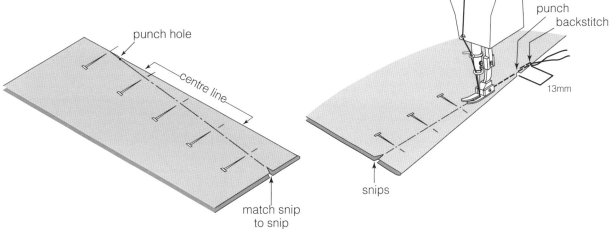

punch hole

centre line

match snip to snip

punch
backstitch

13mm

snips

5   Following the stitchline exactly, continue to stitch the dart from the narrow end to the wide end (toward the snips). Backstitch and clip the threads.

6   Press the dart excess toward the centre or down. Press from the wrong side only. Use a tailor's ham to build shape in the dart area. Refer to Chapter 1 for detailed pressing techniques.

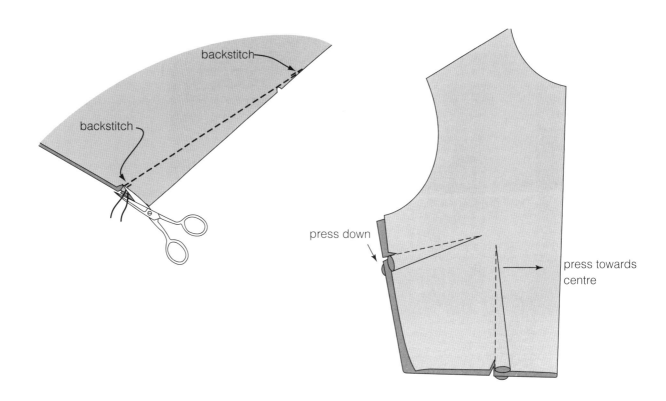

backstitch

backstitch

press down

press towards centre

STUDIO TIP

When pressing, place a strip of paper between the dart and the fabric to prevent an impression from appearing on the correct side of the garment.

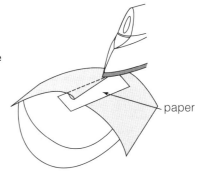

paper

Shaped Tapered Dart

The **shaped tapered dart** is a single dart that allows a more contoured fit in a torso bodice or a halter bodice made in woven fabrics. This dart is usually located in the side seam area and referred to as a French dart.

TRANSFERRING SHAPED TAPERED DART MARKINGS

Transfer dart markings from the pattern to the wrong side of the fabric by following the pencil method.

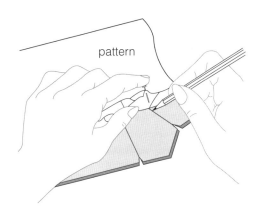

pattern

1 With the correct sides of the fabric together, fold the dart so that the snip ends match. Continue to fold the dart (along the centre line) to the pencil mark or punch hole, making sure that the shape of the dart is maintained exactly.

2 If necessary, pin and pencil in the stitchline.

3 Start to sew (and backstitch) the dart 13mm beyond the punch hole or pencil mark (this is to ensure that the hole is caught). Make sure the needle enters the fabric exactly on the fold at the stitchline for a couple of stitches.

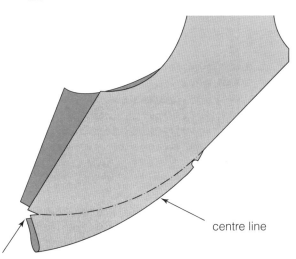

centre line

match snip to snip

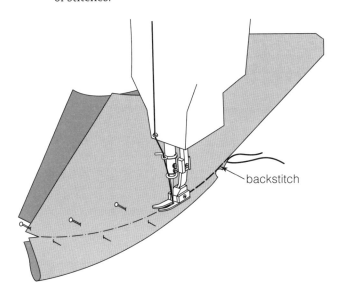

backstitch

4 Following the stitchline exactly, continue to stitch the dart from the narrow to the wide end (towards the snips). Backstitch and clip the threads.

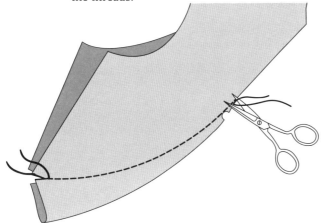

6 Press dart excess toward the centre or down. Press from the wrong side only. Use a tailor's ham to build in the dart area.

5 Clip excess of fold to relieve strain, allowing dart to curve smoothly.

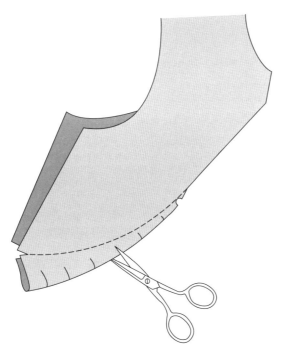

STUDIO TIP

When pressing, place a strip of paper between the dart and the fabric to prevent an impression from appearing on the correct side of the garment.

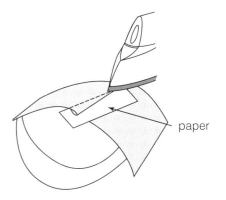

paper

Cut-away Dart

A **cut-away dart** is used in garments that require extremely wide darts (primarily bodice fronts). A cut-away dart reduces bulk in the finished dart area because the excess amount in the middle of the dart has been cut away. This style of dart is used in woven fabric blouses and dresses that have large shaped darts. The dart is stitched in a seam and then pressed.

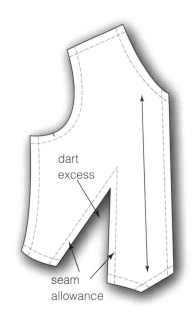

dart excess

seam allowance

TRANSFERRING CUT-AWAY DART MARKINGS

Transfer dart markings from the pattern to the wrong side of the fabric:

A Eliminate the dart excess by cutting along the cutting line of the pattern.

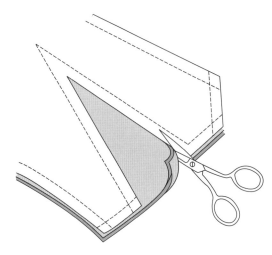

B Snip the ends of the dart lines.
C Punch a hole or pencil mark 13mm before the end of the dart tip.

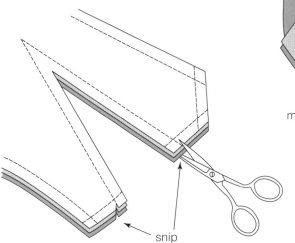

snip

snip

1 With the correct sides of the fabric together, fold the dart so that the snip ends match. Continue to fold the dart, following the seam allowance of the dart to the punch hole or pencil mark.

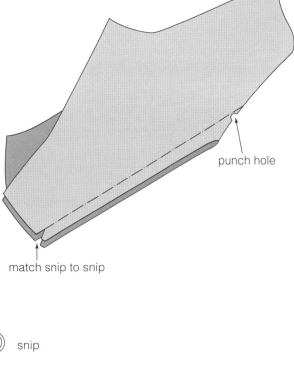

punch hole

match snip to snip

2 If necessary, pin the fabric and pencil in
   the stitchline.

3 Start to sew (and backstitch) the dart 13mm
   beyond the punch hole or pencil mark to
   ensure that the hole is caught.

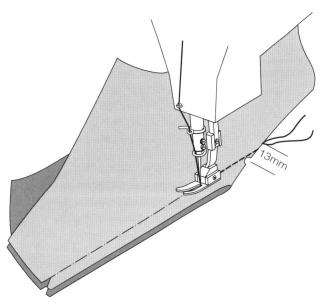

4 Following the seam allowance and the
   stitchline exactly, continue to stitch the
   dart toward the widest end and the snips.
   Backstitch and clip the threads.

5 Press the dart excess open, over
   a tailor's ham.

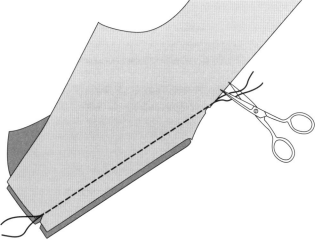

Fisheye Dart

A **fisheye dart** is a double-ended dart formed to fit the body contour at the waistline area. This dart varies in size and length.

TRANSFERRING FISHEYE DART MARKINGS

Transfer dart markings from the pattern to the wrong side of the fabric:

A Place a pin through the pattern and both layers of the fabric 13mm from each end of the dart. Mark with a pencil or punch a hole with an awl.

inside   outside

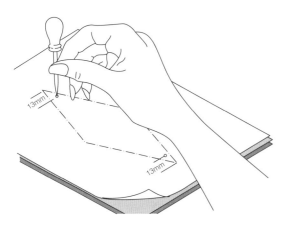

B Pencil mark (or punch a hole) at the centre of the dart and 3mm in from the widest point of the dart.

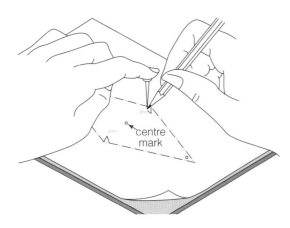

centre mark

1 With the correct sides of the fabric together, fold the crease of the dart so that the top, bottom and centre marks are in one continuous fold. This is the centre of the dart.

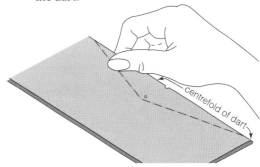

centrefold of dart

2 Start to sew from 13mm beyond the top mark to 3mm beyond the centre mark, to 13mm beyond the bottom mark.

3 Press the dart with the wrong side of the fabric up. Snip the fold at the centre of the dart. Press the finished dart toward the centre of the garment.

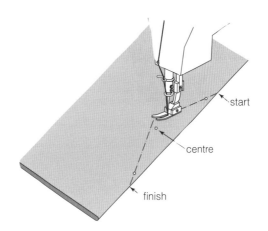

start

centre

finish

PLEATS

A **pleat** is folded excess fabric at the edge of a garment. It is created by doubling the fabric ply on itself, producing a fold and forming an underlay of 16–50mm.

Pleats can be used:

- Singularly or in a series
- At the waist, shoulder, or hipline
- Below a bodice yoke seam or skirt yoke seam
- To fit the lower edge of a sleeve into a cuff
- At a sleeve cap as a design feature
- On a blouse, bodice or jacket to release fullness over the bust or across the shoulder

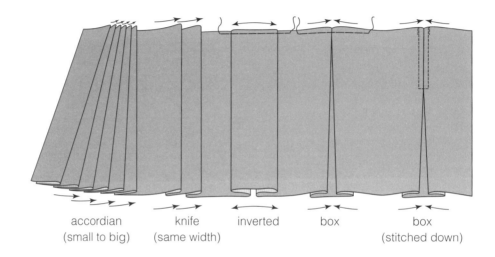

accordian (small to big) knife (same width) inverted box box (stitched down)

Pleats are either pressed or unpressed. They could be folded into place and stitched at the seam or pressed and then stitched to one side. They create a softened effect at points of release, which aids in fitting the garment over body curves.

A **soft pleat** is an **unpressed pleat** that does not have the pleat crease line pressed in place. This creates a rather soft effect, such as in the lower edge of the sleeve and in skirt waistlines.

Pressed pleats have the crease line firmly pressed in position the entire length of the pleat. They may be evenly spaced pressed folds or part of a seam, stitched, and pressed in place.

The most common types of pressed pleats are:
- Accordian pleat
- Box pleat
- Crystal pleat
- Inverted pleat
- Kick pleat
- Knife pleat
- Stitched-down pleat

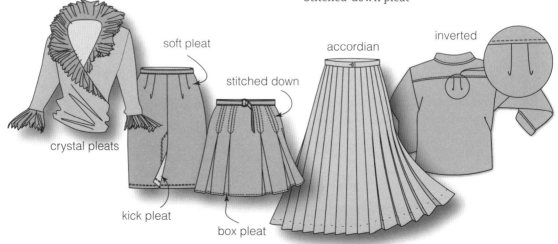

crystal pleats soft pleat stitched down accordian inverted kick pleat box pleat

Knife Pleat

A **knife pleat** is a fabric ply pressed in a series of folds. These are permanently pressed to lie in one direction. Pleats may be planned in groups or as an evenly spaced series around the circumference of a garment.

Each pleat in the pattern is marked with two vertical lines from the waistline or a style line to the lower edge. One line designates the top fold of the pleat, and the other designates the position of the fold forming the pleat. Each pleat is made proportionately deeper at the waistline or style line.

TRANSFERRING KNIFE PLEAT MARKINGS

A Snip the ends of each pleat.
B Pull the pattern away from the fabric. Using a ruler and chalk or pencil, mark the pleat lines, using the snips as a guide.

OR

Mark the fold lines with a hand thread basting stitch. Take small stitches every 7.6cm. Clip the thread between stitches. Use one colour thread for the fold line and another colour for the placement line.

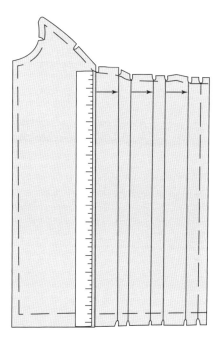

STUDIO TIP

The lower edge of a knife-pleated garment may be hemmed before forming the pleats; this makes the hemming process much easier. The finished length of the garment must be known when using this technique.

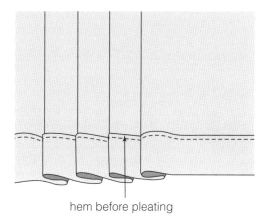

hem before pleating

1 Form each pleat by folding the fabric along each fold line, bringing the fold over to meet the placement line. Pin and baste each pleat the length of the fold.

2 Baste across the top of the pleated section to hold the pleats in place.

3 Press pleats from the correct side, using a pressing cloth. Press lightly for a soft look. Use more pressure for a sharp finish. Turn the garment over and press again.

4 Attach the adjoining garment piece (for example, bodice, yoke or waistband).

PLEAT VARIATION

To make stitched-down pleats, topstitch close to the folded edge, from the hem to where the pleat is to be stitched to the skirt.

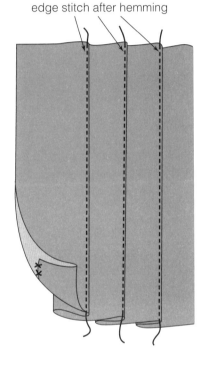

edge stitch after hemming

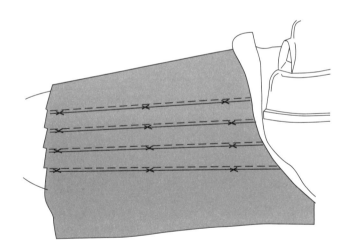

Box Pleat

A box pleat has two folds of equal width turned towards each other, forming two unpressed soft pleats that add extra fullness in a garment section. The pleats are secured by stitching across the folded end. The box pleat is located in yoke style lines, waist seams of trousers or skirts and the lower edge of sleeves.

1   With the correct sides of the fabric facing up, crease both pleat fold lines to each other, meeting at the centre.

2   Baste across the top of the pleated section to hold the pleats in place.

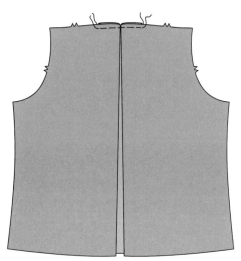

3   Press the pleat flat.

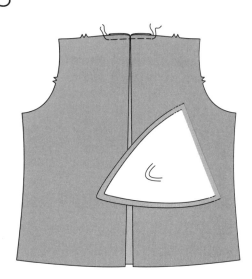

In-seam Pleat

An **in-seam pleat** is an extra fabric ply added to the seam, usually lengthwise, pressed and held in place by topstitching. After the seam is stitched, different styles of pleats are created by the direction of the pressed pleat:

- **Box pleat** – spaced folds doubled over to face away from each other.
- **Inverted pleat** – spaced folds doubled over to face each other (opposite direction of the box pleat).
- **Kick pleat** – spaced folds pressed in one direction.

1   With the correct sides of the fabric together, match the pleat seams to each other.

2   Machine stitch a regular stitch from the top of the seam to the bottom of the pleat seam.

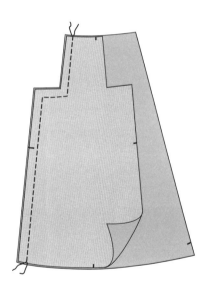

3   Press the seam allowance and the pleat in the direction desired for the pleat.

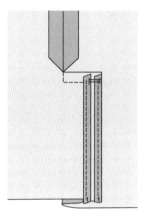

4   On the correct side of the garment, topstitch or edge stitch.

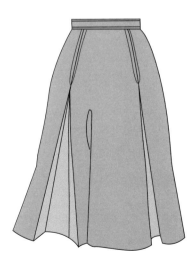

TUCKS

A **tuck** is the take-up of excess fabric of
a determined amount, at the edge of the garment
and converging toward a point or points of release.

There are two basic styles of tuck:
- Dart tuck
- Pin tuck

Dart tucks are used to control and release fullness
as well as to create design details. **Pin tucks** are
evenly spaced parallel folds, 6mm or less, and
stitched to be released. Both styles can be formed
on the inside or outside of the garment.

Tucks can be used:
- To hold fullness in place or for a decorative effect.
- On the front bodice at the waistline, shoulder or
  centre front to release fabric to conform to the
  bust shape.
- On the back bodice at the waistline or shoulder,
  to release fabric to conform to the body contour.
- On the waistline of a skirt, trousers or shorts, to
  allow ease over the hips and abdomen.
- On one-piece garments at the waistline, to
  release fullness above and below a fitted area.
- Instead of darts, to create a softer design effect.

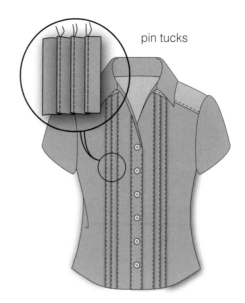

pin tucks

Release Tuck

Release tucks are used to control fullness and then release it at a desired point, such as at the bust or hips. Fullness can also be released at both ends of the release tucks. The spacing between the tucks depends on the effect desired in the finished garment. The most common placement for release tucks are at the waist areas of skirts or trousers and the shoulder areas of bodices.

TRANSFERRING RELEASE TUCK MARKINGS

Transfer tuck markings from the pattern to the wrong side of the fabric as follows:

A Snip the ends of the tuck lines.

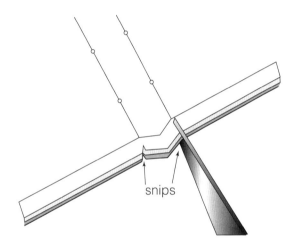

snips

B Place a pin through the pattern and both layers of the fabric. With a pencil, mark the desired stitchline.

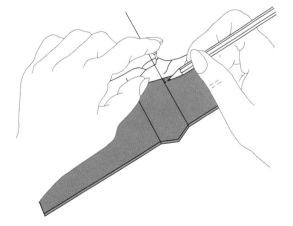

1 With the correct sides of the fabric together, fold the tuck so that the snip ends match.

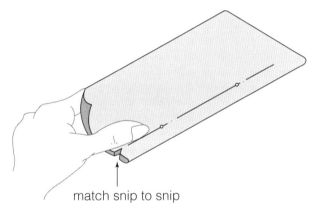

match snip to snip

2 Continue to fold (and pin, if necessary) to the end of the tuck.

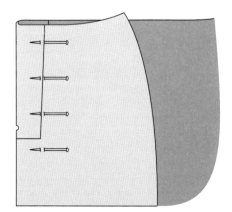

3 Start to sew (and backstitch) from the snipped ends to the release point (the end of the tuck).

5 Press the tucks in the direction desired, usually towards the centre of the garment.

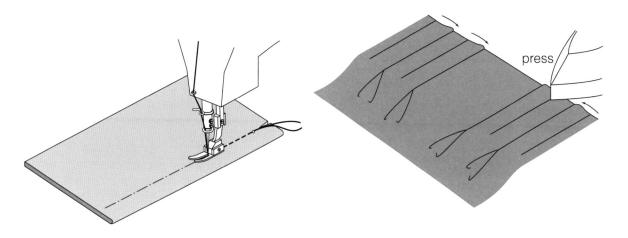

press

4 If desired, stitch across to complete the tuck.

snips

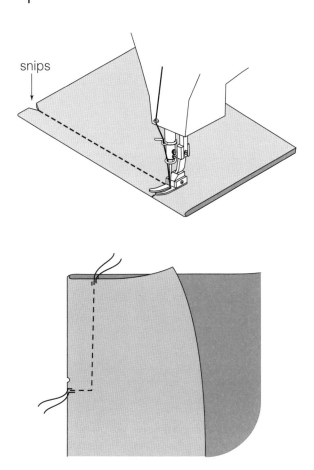

Pin Tuck

Pin tucks are permanently stitched, narrow (usually 3–9mm wide) folds of fabric. By using various tuck widths and lengths, pin tucks can add design interest. They can run the full length of a garment piece or end at various points. Tuck width and spacing between each tuck may vary, depending on the design.

1   Mark the stitching lines of each tuck on the side of the fabric that will be stitched. If the tucks will be stitched from the correct side, use thread basting.

2   Fold and press each tuck, matching stitching lines.

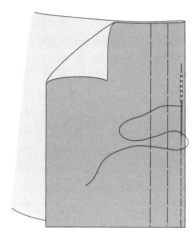

4   Press each tuck flat. Then press each tuck to one side as desired for the design.

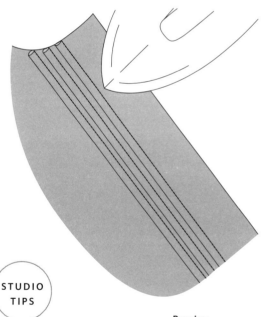

3   Stitch each tuck from the side of the tuck that will be seen. Stitch the tucks along the stitching line, using the fold line of the tuck as a guide.

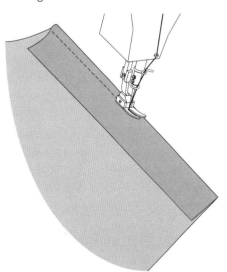

STUDIO TIPS

- Pin tucks can be added to a garment by sewing the tucks into the fabric before cutting out the pattern pieces.
- Sewing machines offer pin tuck feet. These feet are used with a twin needle to create accurate pin tucks.

Bernina Pintuck Foot #30

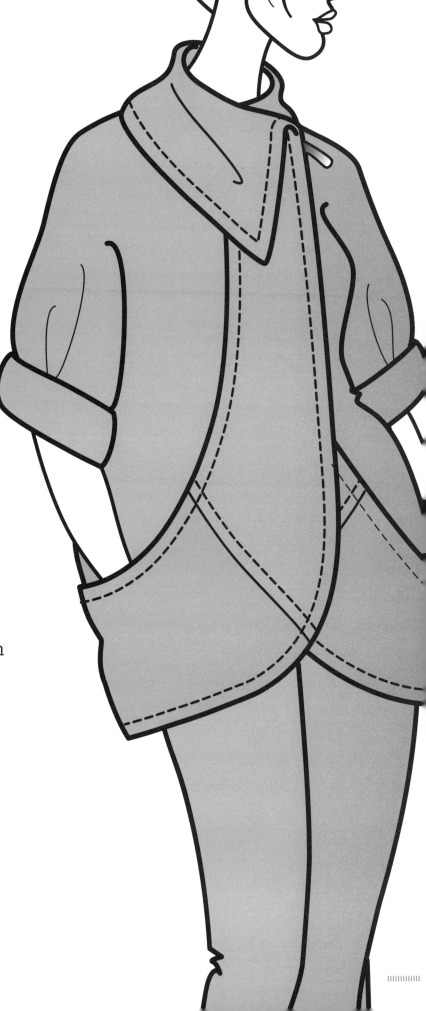

HEMS

- Key Terms and Concepts
- Marking and Turning a Hem
- Rolled or Merrow Hem
- Corner Hem
- Mitred Hem

KEY TERMS *and* CONCEPTS

A **hem** is the finished raw edge at the bottom of a skirt, dress, blouse, sleeve or trousers, which prevents raw edges from fraying or tearing. It is held in place with either hand or machine stitching. The type of hem used depends on the fabric type and garment design. Hems can be:

- turned to the inside of the garment and finished with a hand stitch.
- turned to the outside of the garment as a decorative finish.
- left unturned and finished with a decorative stitch, such as a lettuce stitch.

The **hem allowance** is the extension at the bottom of skirts, dresses, blouses, sleeves and trousers, which is turned under and sewn with an appropriate hemming stitch.

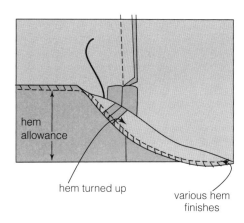

hem allowance

hem turned up

various hem finishes

A **hemline** is the designated line along which the hem is to be folded, faced or finished.

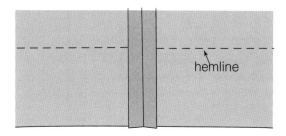

hemline

Hems are secured in place by using a hand or machine stitch, or using a bonding material.

- Machine-stitched hems can be made to show on the outside of the garment.
- Hand stitching (using a variety of different stitches) secures the hem to the inside of the garment and is not visible on the outside of the garment.
- Hems may also be glued as an alternative to either machine stitching or hand stitching.

hand-stitched hem

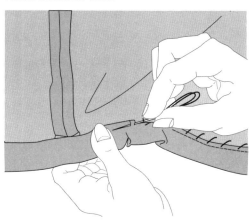

machine-stitched hem

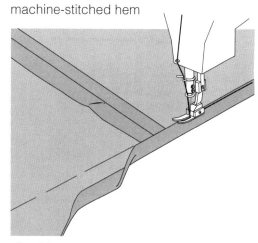

glued hem

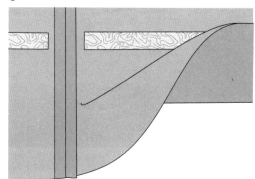

Various decorative hem edges are used to finish the raw edge of the hem. Special hemming devices are sometimes used to duplicate the stitch pattern and appearance of handwork.

The following are some examples of hemming with a special or decorative finish:

- Lettuce edging with a frilled, unturned finished edge can be created by stretching a knit or crinkled fabric as it feeds into an overlocker.
- Faced with a separate piece of fabric.
- Finished with bias binding/tape.
- A merrow or rolled hem finish is produced by overlocking a very narrow finish on the outside edge of the hem.
- A decorative finish can be applied with lace, bias binding, seam tape or netting.
- A wired hem can be produced by incorporating a slender piece of plastic (such as fishing line) into a narrow, folded hem.
- An interfaced hem may be needed for suit jackets, loosely woven fabrics or knits.
- A hand-rolled hem can be used on sheer and delicate fabrics. Roll the fabric between your fingers and then sew it with tiny hand stitches.

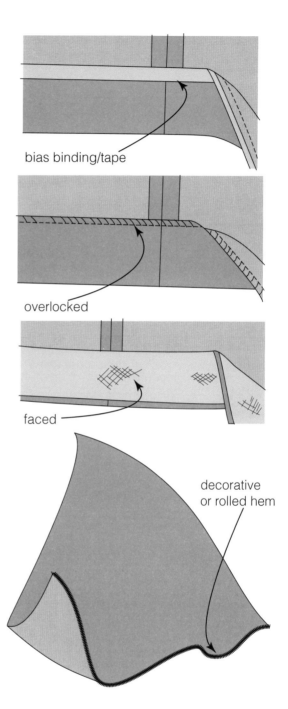

bias binding/tape

overlocked

faced

decorative or rolled hem

MARKING and TURNING A HEM

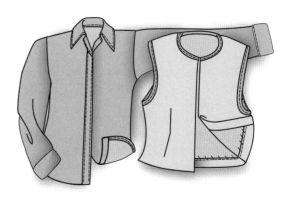

1   The desired length of the garment depends on the fashion for the season, the style of the garment, and personal choice. Mark the hem evenly from the floor to the desired length using a metre rule. If the garment was not carefully made, or if you stand crookedly, the hemline will not measure evenly from the floor.

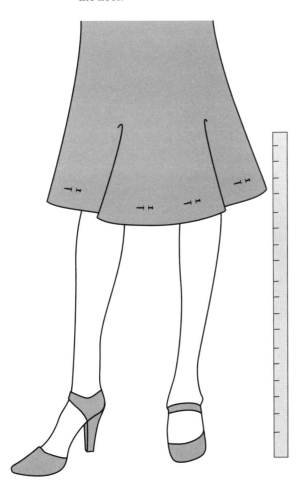

2   After measuring the length at which to hem the garment, measure the desired width of the hem, usually 2.5–3.8cm. Cut off all excess fabric.

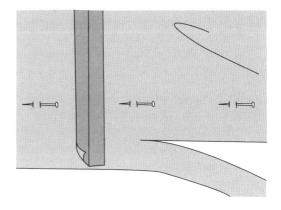

3   The outer edge of the hem should be finished so that it does not ravel. You can sew on bias tape, turn the edge under 6mm and stitch, overlock the outer edge, or hand stitch.

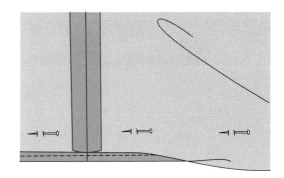

4   With the wrong side of the garment facing you, fold the hem up at the desired position. Pin in place.

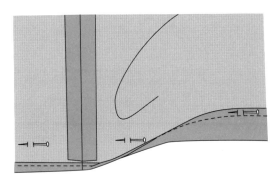

5   Select an appropriate hemming stitch and sew the hem in place. Refer to Hand Hemming Stitches on pages 91–92.

NOTE: If the garment is flared, it will be necessary to reduce hem bulk. Crimp the outer edge of the garment hem and then finish the outer edge. Refer to crimping on page 87.

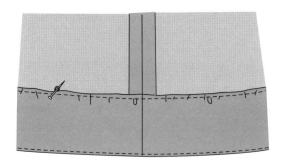

6   After completing the desired hemming stitch, press the hem in place. Make sure the hem is pressed clean and flat from the inside of the garment.

NOTE: To prevent an impression of the hem appearing on the correct side of the garment, place a strip of paper or pressing cloth between the hem and the garment.

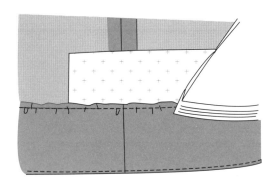

ROLLED *or* MERROW HEM

A **rolled hem** or **merrow hem** is a distinctive stitch made with an overlocker. This hemming stitch is used to clean-finish the hems of skirts and dresses and the raw edge of scarves to give the appearance of a satin finish.

In the fashion industry, a special industrial overlocker is used to produce the merrow edge and domestic overlockers will require a special setting. No additional turning or stitch is required for this hem.

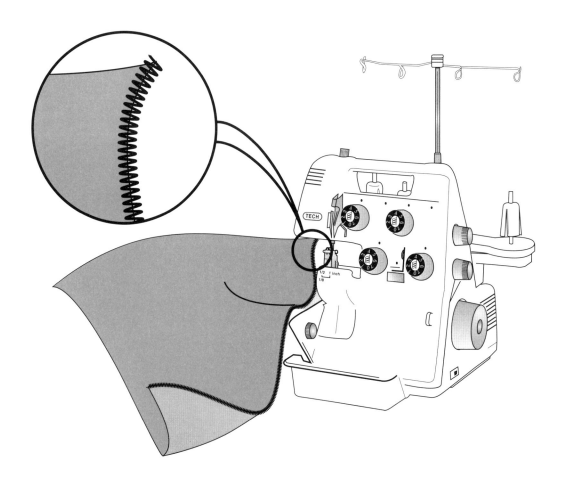

CORNER HEM

A **corner hem** is used to finish the area where
a buttoned front facing meets the bottom of
a blouse, dress, jacket or skirt. The hem of the
garment will automatically be turned up into
position using this technique.

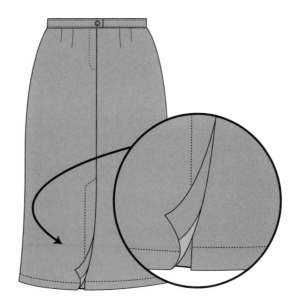

1 Turn back the facing on the garment at
   the required fold line position, correct
   sides together.

2 Machine stitch the facing to the garment at
   the desired hemline position.

3 Trim the corner and turn the facing to the
   wrong side of the garment.

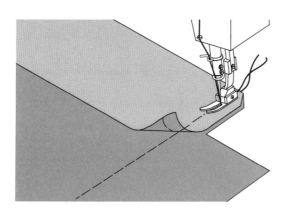

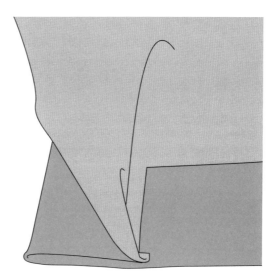

MITRED HEM

A **mitred hem** is used when a sharp square corner with a diagonal line from the corner is desired. Mitred hems can be used on items such as waistcoats, tablecloths and place mats.

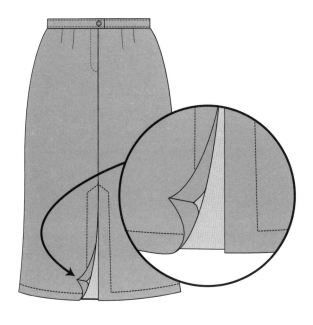

1 Turn back the width of the hem, matching the edges diagonally from the seam allowance (or hem allowance) to the corner. Make sure the correct sides are together.

2 Stitch diagonally from the corner.

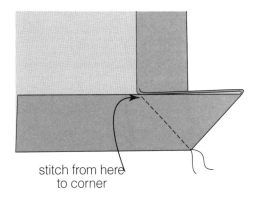

stitch from here to corner

3 Trim away surplus material to 6mm of the stitchline. Press the seam open.

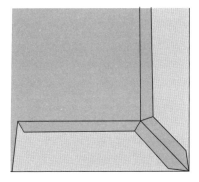

4 Turn the hem to the inside (the wrong side) of the garment. Finish the hem with a hand stitch.

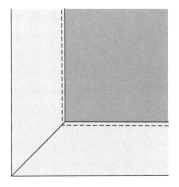

CHAPTER

8

CLOSURES

- Key Terms and Concepts

- Buttons and Buttonholes

- Hook-and-loop Tape

- Hooks and Eyes

- Zips

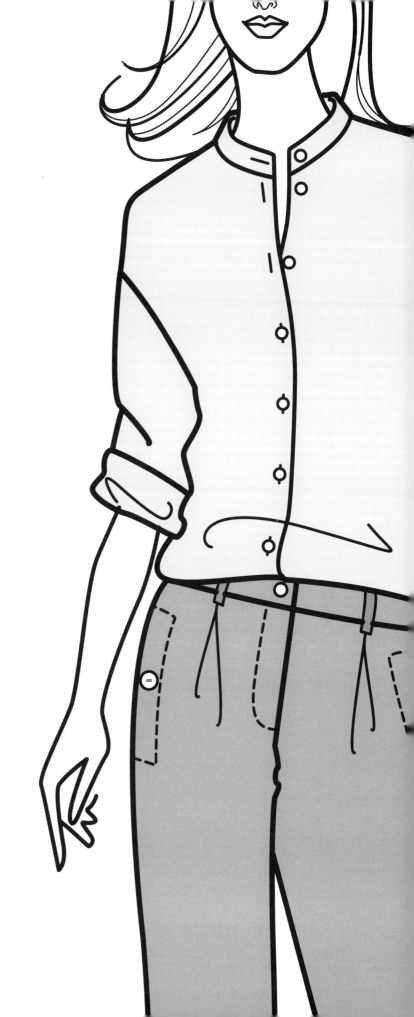

KEY TERMS *and* CONCEPTS

Closures are used to fasten garments securely. They are designed for a variety of holding purposes and can be decorative as well as functional; forming a focal point in a garment design, to enhance the look of the garment. The type of closure selected depends on the design and use of the garment and the weight and type of fabric. Closures include the following:

- **Buttons** are available in a wide variety of natural or manufactured materials, including pearl, wood, bone, fibre, fabric, glass, jewels, plastic, steel and other metals. Buttons can be covered with fabric or other materials to complement a garment. There are two types of buttons:

  ○ The sew-through button has two or four holes for attaching the button to the garment.

 two-hole sew-through

 four-hole sew-through

  ○ The shank button has a metal, fabric, plastic or thread extension under the surface of the button for attaching the button to the garment.

metal shank

cloth shank

thread shank

- **Buckles** come in a variety of sizes and shapes and are used to close tabs or belts.
- **Hooks and eyes** are available in various sizes and styles and are designed as a closing device for garments.

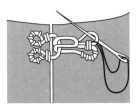

- **Hook-and-loop tape** is composed of two woven nylon strips – one with tiny hooks and one with a looped pile. The hook and loop intermesh when hooked together; available in a variety of sizes, shapes and colours.

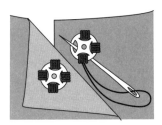

- **Snaps** are circular plates moulded with a mating ball and a socket. They are available in a variety of sizes and are used to fasten a garment area where a smooth, flat closure is desired.
- **Metal eyelets** are small, round metal tubes, with an opening of approximately 6mm used to accommodate lacing and to add a design detail.
- **Zips** are devices for fastening a garment open or closed. A zip is a device made of metal teeth or synthetic coils that make a complete closure by means of interlocking.

STUDIO TIP

Use a sewing gauge to space buttons and buttonholes, pleats and tucks quickly and easily. This expandable gauge stretches to measure any desirable spacing.

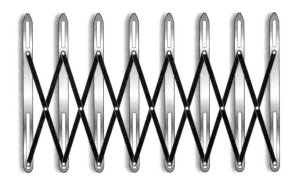

BUTTONS *and* BUTTONHOLES

Buttonholes

A **buttonhole** is a finished opening, sized to accommodate a button. Buttonholes can be used on any edge that overlaps, such as a cuff, waistband or blouse. There are three types of buttonholes:

A Machine-worked buttonholes are made by using a machine attachment or zigzag stitching.

B Bound buttonholes are made with separate strips of fabric. They are constructed before facings are applied.

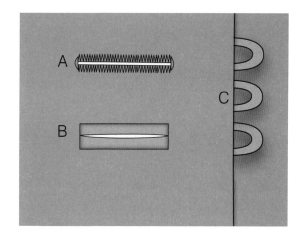

C Loops are made of bias tubing, thread or cording. They are placed to extend beyond the edge of the garment in lieu of the extension of the garment.

Buttonhole Placement

Buttonholes are placed on the right-hand side of the garment openings of women's or children's clothing, and on the left-hand side of men's and boys' clothing. Buttonholes are usually placed in a horizontal direction, except on shirt plackets, where they are usually placed vertically.

Some sewing machines have buttonhole attachments. It is important to refer to the manual provided with the sewing machine for directions on the correct use of the attachment. Buttonholes can also be made using the zigzag stitch on the sewing machine.

A pattern will suggest the position of buttonholes. The spacing can be adjusted to suit your adaptation of the garment design.

Mark the width of the button for a horizontal and vertical buttonhole on the centre-front line with a chalk pencil.

Horizontal buttonholes are placed 3mm beyond the centre line of the garment and extend (the length of the button) into the garment (not into the extension area).

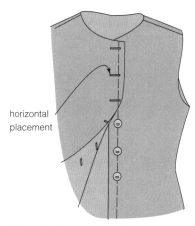

horizontal placement

Vertical buttonholes are placed on the centre line (not the edge) of the garment or placket. The vertical spacing is determined by the design of the garment.

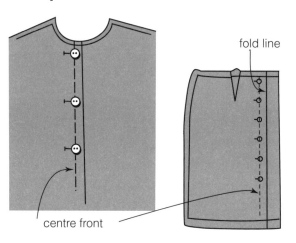

fold line

centre front

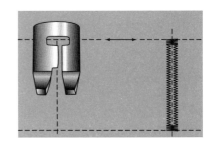

Machine-worked Buttonholes

Machine-worked buttonholes can be made even if the sewing machine does not have a buttonhole attachment, as long as it has a zigzag feature. Attach the zigzag throat plate and zigzag presser foot to the sewing machine. Adjust the stitch length to its smallest setting and adjust the zigzag width to the middle setting.

1 Working on the correct side of the garment, insert the machine needle into the fabric at one end of the buttonhole. Slowly zigzag stitch the length of the desired buttonhole. Complete this stitch with the needle down and on the side of the buttonhole opening.

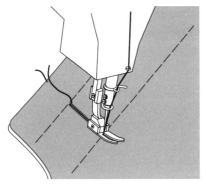

2 With the needle down, raise the presser foot and pivot the garment completely around.

3 Raise the needle position and adjust the zigzag width to the widest setting. Stitch about five times at the end of the buttonhole; this is called a **bartack**.

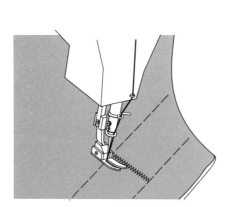

4 Raise the needle position and adjust the zigzag width to the middle section. Stitch the other side of the buttonhole, the length of the buttonhole.

5 Raise the needle position and adjust the zigzag width to the widest setting. Stitch this end about five times to create another bartack.

6 Open the buttonhole by cutting through the middle of the stitches using a seam ripper or sharp scissors.

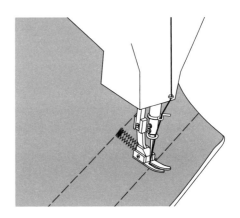

Buttonhole Loops

Buttonhole loops are made of bias tubing. They extend beyond the edge of the garment instead of including an extension on the garment.

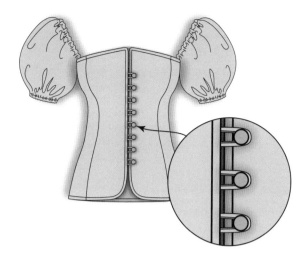

1 The bias tubing must be long enough to cut into as many loops as necessary. Each loop must be long enough to fit over the button and provide a seam allowance on each end.

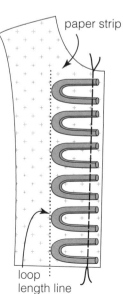

2 Loop the finished tubing around the desired button to calculate the amount of loop needed for the button.

3 Make a copy of the facing out of shelf paper. Note the stitchline. Draw in a second line that shows the width of the loop needed. This ensures that each button loop will be exactly the same size.

4 Stitch the loops to the paper pattern. Start stitching at the top of the pattern. Form loops pointing away from the edge, matching the outer edge and the second line. Stitch the loops on the seamline, one at a time.

5 Pin the paper pattern with the attached loops on top of the correct side of the garment. Pin the facing over the paper pattern.

6 Stitch along the seamline. Trim the ends of the loops to reduce thickness. Tear away the paper pattern.

7 Trim the seam allowance and turn the facing to the inside. Press the facing, extending the loops away from the garment.

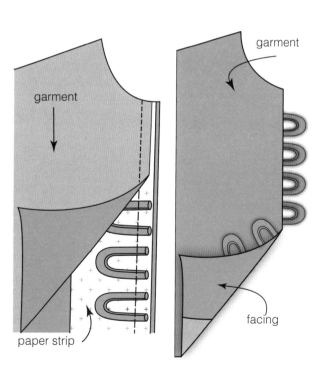

paper strip

loop length line

garment

garment

paper strip

facing

Placing Buttons

It is important that the size of the button fits the buttonhole. An accurate button size will prevent the garment from twisting or pulling.

To mark the position of the buttons, start at the neck edge or top of the garment and match the centre of the garment along the centre-front line. Pin the garment closed. Place a pin through the centre position of the desired buttonhole. Mark the pinned position on the button side.

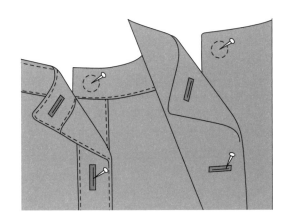

Sewing Flat Buttons

A shank will be constructed while the button is being attached to prevent the garment from pulling at the buttonhole location.

1   Repeatedly draw the thread through one hole of the button (from the wrong side) and down through the opposite hole (from the correct side of the button) into the fabric.

2   Slip a straight pin underneath the thread on the correct side of the button. Continue to follow the stitching process in step 1, repeating the stitches several times.

3   Remove the straight pin from the button and slightly pull the button away from the garment. This will leave a shank, created by the thread between the garment and the button. Wind the thread tightly around this thread shank to complete the process. Knot and cut the thread at the base of the shank.

Sewing Shank Buttons

Shank buttons are recommended as closures on heavyweight garments such as coats. An additional shank is sewn when attaching a shank button to the garment, similar to the procedure used to create a shank for a flat button.

1   Make a couple of small stitches at the marking for the button on the garment.

2   Repeatedly bring the thread through the shank of the button and back into the fabric. While sewing the shank, hold the button away from the garment about a finger's width. Stitch using this method for about six stitches.

3   While holding the button away from the garment, wind the thread tightly around the shank created by the thread. Knot and cut the thread at the base of the shank.

HOOK-AND-LOOP TAPE

Hook-and-loop tape (commonly known by its commercial name, Velcro) is a substitute for zips, buttons and adjustable waistlines on garments for men, women and children. Hook-and-loop tape is available in many widths and colours. One layer of the tape has a hook side and the other layer has a loop side. When these two layers are pressed together, they lock into place until pulled apart.

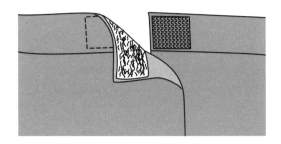

1   Position the hook layer of the tape on the bottom garment piece. Edge stitch around the entire piece.

2   Position the loop portion of the tape on the overlapping portion of the garment. Edge stitch around the entire piece.

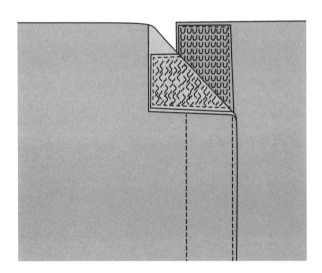

HOOKS AND EYES

Hooks and eyes are available in a variety of sizes and types. The type selected is determined by the type of closure and the position on the garment, such as at the top of a zip closure on waistbands or necklines.

The general-purpose hook with a straight eye or round eye is the most commonly used. The special-purpose hook and eye is used primarily for waistbands.

1 Position and stitch the hook first, using overhand stitches. Stitch around the hook and through the fabric, being careful not to allow the stitches to show on the other side of the garment. Then stitch across the end of the hook.

2 Close the garment and put a mark or pin where the hook meets the other garment section. Position the eye and stitch around each end of the eye, again using overhand stitches.

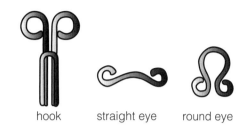

hook   straight eye   round eye

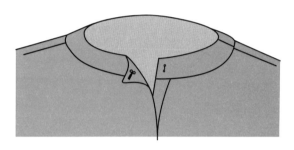

general-purpose hook with straight eye

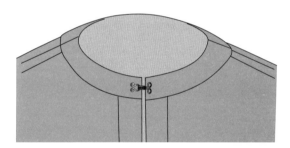

general-purpose hook with round eye

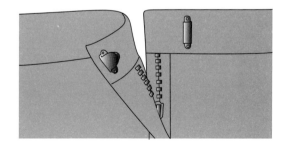

special-purpose hook and eye

ZIPS

A **zip** is a fastening device made with metal teeth
or synthetic coils that make a complete closure by
interlocking. Zips provide a convenient access for
opening and closing a garment. There are several
types and lengths of zip closures available, and
a variety of methods can be used to insert them.
The type selected depends on the location of the
zip in the garment, the type of fabric and the
garment design.

Today's zips are offered in several different styles
and for various fabric weights and types. Shown
here are an invisible zip with a special fabric tape for
sheers, a rhinestone zip, leather zips and a lace zip
for lace fabrics.

There are three basic types of zips:

The **conventional zip** opens at the top and has a
stop at the bottom. This style is available in a variety
of lengths and is used for garment styles that
require a top opening and a bottom closure. This zip
is used on:

- Skirt and neckline openings
- Trousers and shorts
- The finished edges of fitted sleeves
- The centre seam of a hood to convert a hood to
  a collar
- Long sleeve openings
- Horizontally for design detail, such as on pockets

conventional zip

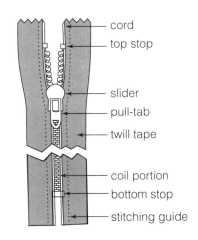

- cord
- top stop
- slider
- pull-tab
- twill tape
- coil portion
- bottom stop
- stitching guide

The **invisible zip** is similar to the conventional zip but with special coils to conceal it in the seam. It is applied using a special sewing foot. The invisible zip is used:

- Where any other zip application would detract from the finished appearance of the garment, such as on matt jersey, velvet or lace
- To give a smooth, continuous seamline
- On the lower edge openings of fitted sleeves

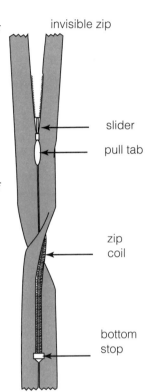

invisible zip

slider

pull tab

zip coil

bottom stop

The **separating zip** is open at both ends. This type is available in lightweight to heavyweight coils and can be inserted as a decorative zip where tape and teeth will show on the face of the garment or be concealed beneath the seam folds. This zip is available in a variety of lengths. The separating zip is used:

- Wherever two sections of a garment separate completely, such as on a jacket, coat or parka
- On detachable hoods
- To separate linings from dual-season coats and jackets
- On snowsuits and leggings
- As a design detail

separating zip

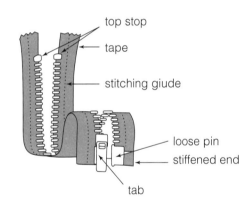

top stop

tape

stitching giude

loose pin

stiffened end

tab

Zip Feet

An **adjustable zip foot** for home machines is a single-toed presser foot that is notched on both sides. It is designed with a shank that is fixed to an adjustable horizontal slide bar to accommodate the needle and facilitate stitching for left and right construction, close to the raised edges of a zip.

A **half zip foot** or **slit foot** for industrial machines has a narrow, two-toed base to accommodate the needle. This foot permits sewing close to the raised edge of the zip teeth or coil. It is used in applications for heavyweight fabrics, or any centred, lapped or fly-front zip insertion.

A **cording foot** is a metal presser foot, notched on one side only, to permit sewing close to the raised edge of zip teeth or coil. Some sewers prefer to use the cording foot instead of the adjustable zip foot.

Preparing a Sewing Machine with a Zip Foot

For all zip applications, attach the zip foot to the sewing machine. Position the foot so that the needle is to the side of the zip being sewn – usually the right side. On an industrial machine, use the half foot to insert zips.

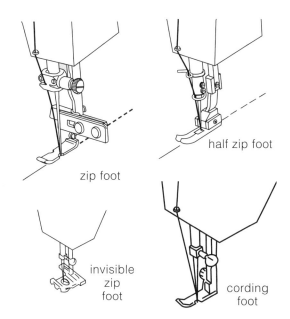

zip foot

half zip foot

invisible
zip
foot

cording
foot

Zip Applications

There are several methods of inserting zips, depending on the placement of the zip in the garment, the type of zip and the type of garment.

Popular zip applications are:
- **Hand-stitched** zip application, which is used on sheer or couture fabrics or garments not subject to heavy wear or frequent laundering.
- **Railroad** or **centred** zip application, which is used on centre-front or centre-back seams at a neckline or waistline.
- **Lapped** zip application, which is used on necklines of dresses and back openings of skirts and trousers.
- **Fly-front** or **mock fly** zip application, which is used on trousers.
- **Invisible** zip application, which is concealed in the seam and applied using a special sewing foot and instructions.

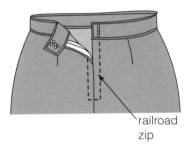

railroad zip

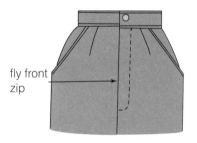

fly front zip

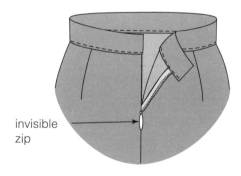

invisible zip

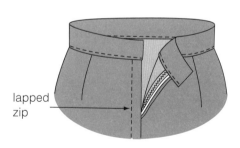

lapped zip

Railroad or Centred Zip Application

The **railroad or centred zip application** is the most common type. It is used in centre-front or centre-back seams at a neckline or waistline. The stitching is visible on both sides of the zip and is an equal distance from the centre. With the basted seam method, the zip is inserted and the zip seam allowance is sewn together with a basting stitch.

1   Baste stitch the seamline for the zip opening. Press the seam allowance open.

NOTE: Home sewing patterns usually allow a 16mm seam allowance for zips. Industry patterns allow a 19–25mm seam allowance.

2   Open the zip and place the correct side of the zip to the wrong side of the garment, with the zip teeth against the basted seamline. Pin in place.

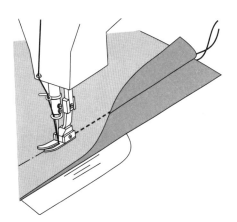

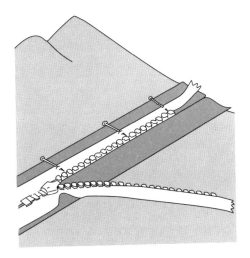

3 Starting from the top edge of the garment and 9mm away from the zip teeth, stitch just beyond the bottom of the zip.

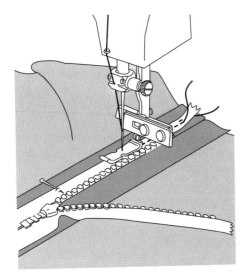

4 With the needle down, lift the presser foot and pivot the garment so that the bottom of the zip can be sewn. Close the zip at this time.

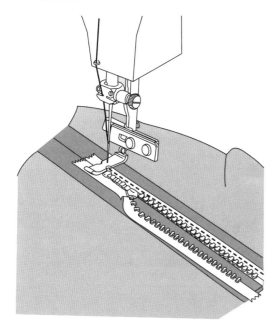

5 Lower the presser foot against the zip and stitch across the bottom.

6 Once again, with the needle down, lift the presser foot and pivot the garment. Stitch along the other side of the zip, 9mm away from the zip teeth, to the top edge of the garment.

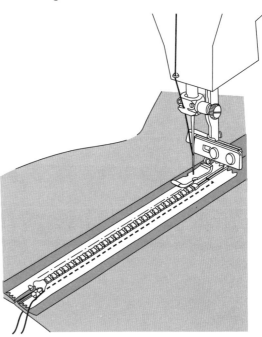

7 Carefully remove the basting stitches, and press the completed zip area.

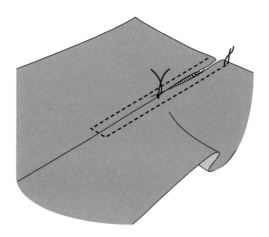

Lapped Zip Application

The lapped zip application conceals the zip with a fold of the fabric. Only one row of stitching is visible on the correct side of the garment. The lapped zip application method is especially suitable for neckline zips on dresses and back openings on skirts and trousers.

1   Machine stitch the seam up to the zip opening.

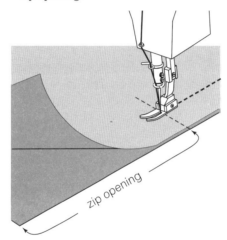

zip opening

2   Press open the seam allowance needed for the zip.

NOTE: Home sewing patterns usually allow a 16mm seam allowance for zips. Industry patterns allow a 19–25mm seam allowance.

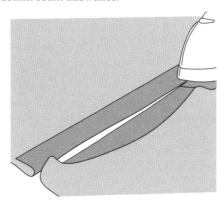

3   Working on the left seam allowance, slide out and pin this seam allowance 3–6mm beyond the pressed seamline.

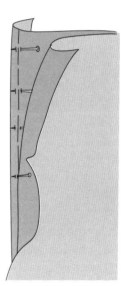

4   With the zip closed and the correct side of the zip and fabric area facing up, position one edge of the zip teeth next to the folded extended seam allowance. Pin in place.

NOTE: The zip tape extends into the seam allowance on the upper edge of the garment.

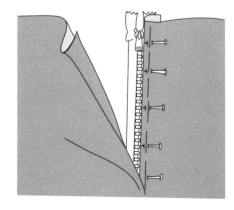

5 Using a zip foot and starting from the bottom of the zip, stitch close to the folded edge of the seam allowance for the entire length of the zip.

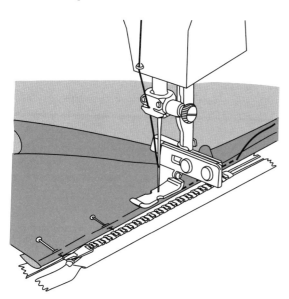

7 Machine stitch 13mm away from and parallel to the seam fold, through all layers of fabric and the zip tape, and across the bottom of the zip.

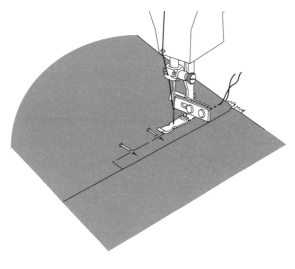

6 With the correct side of the garment facing up, pin the other seam allowance over the closed zip so that it conceals the zip and the other stitching.

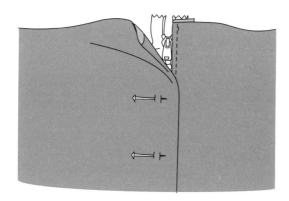

VARIATION FINAL STITCH

To complete the final stitch, open the zip and, using a marking on the throat plate as a guide, machine stitch from the top of the zip to within 25mm of the bottom. With the needle down, lift the presser foot and close the zip. Lower the presser foot and stitch to the end of the zip and across the bottom.

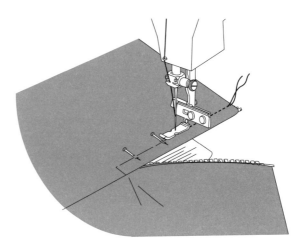

Mock Fly-front Zip Application

The mock fly-front zip application is most often used as a front closing for trousers and some skirts. This is the less complicated method of inserting a fly-front zip.

Preparing Pattern Pieces

The pattern pieces will have an extended shaped seam allowance (3.8cm fly extension) where the zip will be inserted.

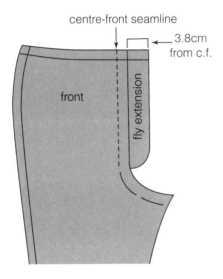

centre-front seamline

3.8cm from c.f.

front

fly extension

1   Stitch the crotch seam to the zip opening (the bottom of the fly extension). Clip at the bottom of the fly extension.

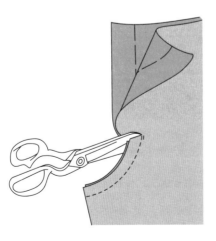

2   Press open the fly extension along the centre-front line.

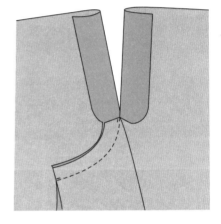

3   Slide out and pin the right fly extension 3–6mm beyond the pressed centre-front line. This additional 3–6mm must extend the entire length of the zip opening.

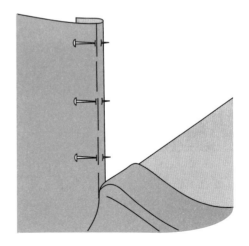

4 With the zip closed and the correct side of the zip and fabric facing up, position one edge of the zip teeth next to the folded extended side. Pin in place. The zip tape extends into the seam allowance on the upper edge of the garment.

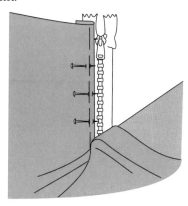

5 Using a zip foot and starting from the bottom of the zip, stitch close to the folded edge of the seam allowance.

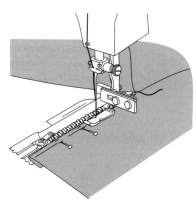

6 With the correct side of the garment facing up, pin the other folded fly-extension seam allowance over the closed zip so that it conceals the zip and the other stitching.

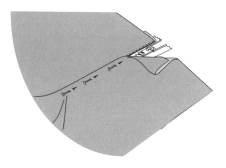

7 With the wrong side of the garment facing up, flip the garment back to expose the unsewn fly extension and zip tape. Sew the zip tape to the fly extension. Keep the garment free of this area so that this stitching will not go through the garment.

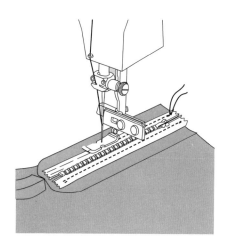

8 Turn the garment to the correct side. Machine stitch 19mm away from and parallel to the fly fold, through all the layers of fabric, curving to meet the bottom of the zip.

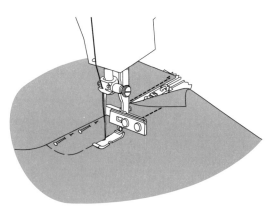

Fly-front Zip Application

The fly-front zip application uses a more tailored detail and is used in both women's and men's fly-front opening trousers, especially dress trousers and jeans.

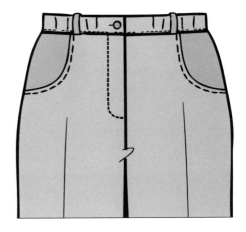

Preparing Pattern Pieces

Prepare a separate zip-facing piece that is 3.8cm wide (on the fold) and the length of the zip tape. Then prepare two fly-shield pieces that are 5cm wide and the length of the zip tape.

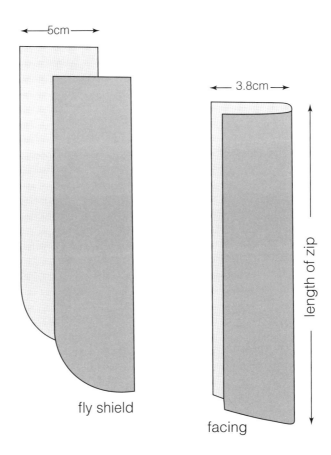

fly shield

facing

1   Stitch the crotch seam up to the zip opening. Clip at the bottom of the fly extension.

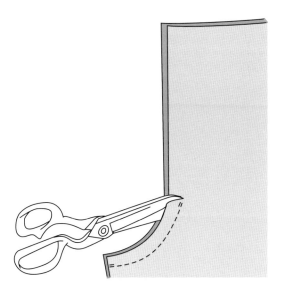

2   Fold the facing piece in half (correct side facing up) and place it to the correct side of the right crotch seam.

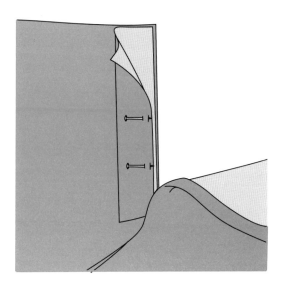

3   Stitch the facing piece to the crotch seam, using a 6mm seam allowance.

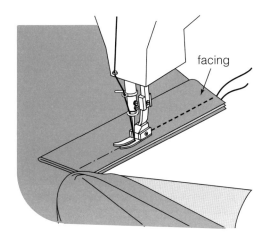

facing

4   Flip the facing away from the trousers and turn the seam allowance to the facing. Top stitch 3mm away from the seamline.

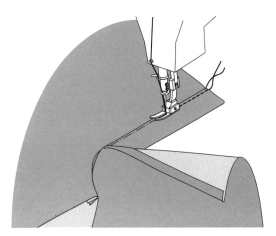

Fly-front Zip Application (Continued)

5   Prepare the fly shield pieces by stitching the curved edges together, with a 6mm seam allowance.

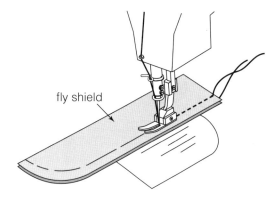

fly shield

6   Turn the fly shield pieces to the outside and press.

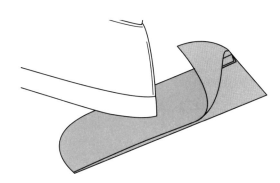

7   With the wrong side of the zip facing up, place the zip between the prepared fly shield and the correct side of the crotch seam. Pin in place.

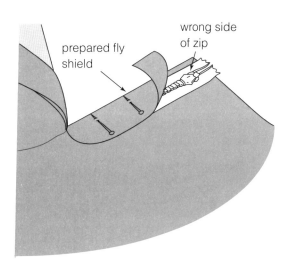

prepared fly shield

wrong side of zip

8   Using the zip foot, stitch through all the layers of fabric and the zip tape, the entire length of the fly shield.

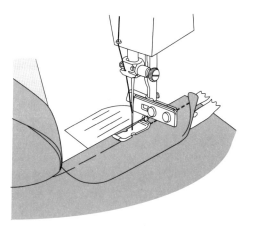

9 Lay the correct side of the trousers facing up on the sewing table, with the zip closed and the fly shield and zip flipped away from the trousers. Edge stitch the zip seam for reinforcement.

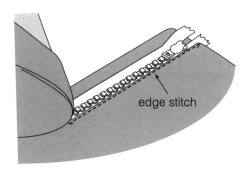

edge stitch

10 In this position, pin the other crotch seam (with the attached facing folded under) over the closed zip so that the zip is concealed.

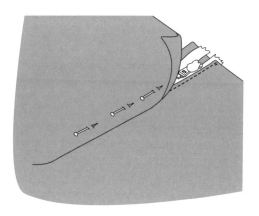

11 Turn the trousers to the wrong side. Flip the garment back to expose the facing and the zip. Sew the zip tape to the facing. Keep the garment and the fly shield free of this area so that this stitching will not go through the garment.

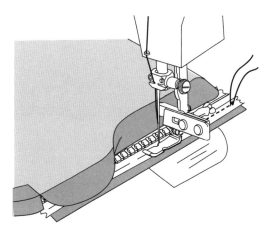

12 Turn the garment to the correct side. Hold the fly away from the zip and keep the pinning in position. Machine 19mm away from and parallel to the seam, through all the layers of fabric, curving in at the bottom of the opening.

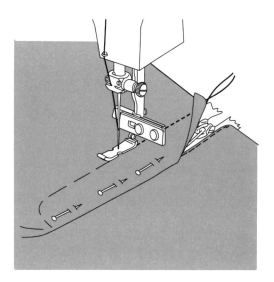

Invisible Zip Application

The invisible zip is used instead of a conventional zip if it is desirable to retain the look of a plain seam (for example, on an evening gown), where the zip stitching would spoil the line of the garment.

NOTE: A special zip foot attachment is required to insert an invisible zip. This special attachment can be purchased at most fabric stores.

NOTE: The invisible zip is inserted before the two garment pieces are sewn together and before the top edge is faced or finished.

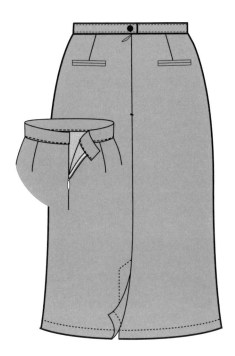

1   Press the zip so that the coils stand away from the tape.

2   Open the invisible zip and place it on the left garment piece, on the correct side of the fabric, with the wrong side of the zip facing up. The zip teeth are placed along the stitchline and the zip tape toward the outer edge of the seam allowance. Baste in place.

3   Place the left-hand groove of the zip foot over the coils of the zip. Roll the coil away from the zip tape and slowly stitch the zip to the fabric until the foot touches the pull tab.

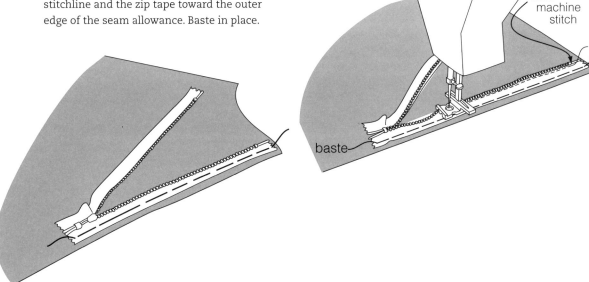

4 Close the zip and place both the right and left garment pieces on top of each other, matching correct sides and zip stitchlines. Baste in place.

HINT: To help position the zip correctly, use markings along the zip tape and the seam allowance.

NOTE: The zip teeth should be placed along the stitchline and the zip tape towards the outer edge of the seam allowance.

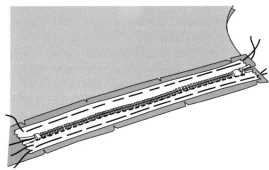

6 Close the zip. Slide the special foot to the left so that the needle is in line with the edge of the foot. The conventional zip foot can be placed on the machine at this time.

7 Place the end of the zip out and away from the seam area. Stitch the garment seam closed along the seamline, from the bottom stitching of the zip to the remainder of the garment seam.

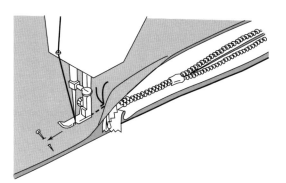

8 Press the seam allowance open and stitch the ends of the zip tapes to the seam allowances.

5 Open the zip and position the right-hand groove of the zip foot over the coils of the zip. Roll the coil away from the zip tape and slowly stitch the second side in place, finishing at the pull tab.

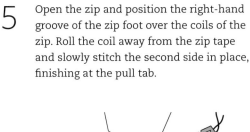

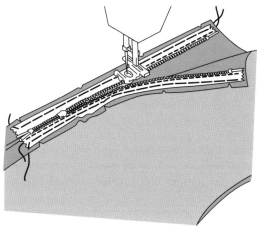

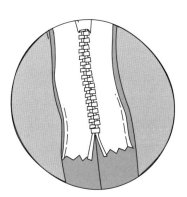

APPENDIX

MACHINE RESOURCES

Reference Books and DVDs for an Overlocker

The following books provide further information on overlockers/sergers:

Bednar, N and van der Kley, A
Creative Serging: Innovative Applications to Get the Most from Your Serger
New York and London: Sterling, 2005

Editors of Creative Publishing International and Singer
The New Sewing with a Serger
Minnetonka, MN: Creative Publishing International, 1999

Griffin, M; Hastings, P; Mercik, A; and Lee, L
Serger Secrets: High Fashion Techniques for Creating Great-Looking Clothes
Emmaus, PA: Rodale Books, 1998

James, C
Complete Serger Handbook
New York: Sterling, 1998

Melot, G
Ready, Set, Serge: Quick and Easy Projects You Can Make in Minutes
Cincinnati, OH: Krause Publications, 2009

Palmer, P and Brown, G
Sewing with Sergers: The Complete Handbook for Overlock Sewing. 3rd edition
Portland, OR: Palmer/Pletsch Publishing, 2004

Young, T
ABCs of Serging: A Complete Guide to Serger Sewing Basics
Radnor, PA: Chilton Book Co., 1992

The following DVDs provide further information on overlockers/sergers:

Alto, M and Palmer, P
Creative Serging
Portland, OR: Palmer/Pletsch, Inc., 2004

Alto, M and Palmer, P
Serger Basics
Portland, OR: Palmer/Pletsch, Inc., 2004

Gabel, M J
Serge and Sew with Mary Jo
Instructional DVDs, Gabel Enterprises, P.O. Box 312, Nipomo, CA 93444

Pullen, M C and McMakin, K
Heirloom Sewing by Serger
Brownsboro, AL: Martha Pullen Co., 2007

Van der Kley, A
Basic Overlocking
Tasmania, Australia: 1800 Sew Help Me, 2005

Manufacturers of Sewing Machines and Overlockers

These manufacturers produce sewing machines and overlockers in a variety of models, with many features and price ranges. UK addresses are given for international companies.

Bernina
91 Goswell Road
London EC1V 7EX
United Kingdom
www.bernina.com

Brother Sewing Machines Europe GmbH UK
Shepley Street, Audenshaw
Manchester M34 5JD
United Kingdom
www.brothersewing.eu

Elna
Elna Centre
Southside, Stockport
Cheshire SK6 2SP
United Kingdom
www.elna.co.uk

Husqvarna Viking
VSM (UK) LTD
Ravensbank House
Ravensbank Drive, Redditch
Worcestershire B98 9NA
United Kingdom
new.husqvarnaviking.com

Janome
Janome Centre
Southside, Stockport
Cheshire SK6 2SP
United Kingdom
www.janome.co.uk

Pfaff Sewing Machines
VSM (UK) Ltd
Ravensbank House
Ravensbank Drive, Redditch
Worcestershire B98 9NA
United Kingdom
www.pfaff.com

Singer
Bogod & Company Ltd
91 Goswell Road,
London EC1V 7EX
United Kingdom
www.singerco.co.uk

Industrial Machine Manufacturers

Contact the industrial sewing machine dealer nearest you to see the following models:

Bernina	Pegasus
Bieffe	Pfaff
Brandless	Seiko
Brother	Singer
Durkopf-Adler	Toyota
Global	Tysew
Juki	Union Special
Mauser-Spezial	

GLOSSARY

Adjustment line: a double line printed on a pattern to indicate where alterations of lengthening or shortening may be made.

A-line: a silhouette shape of a simple dress or skirt, fitted at the top and flared at the hemline, resembling the shape of an A.

Alter: changing a pattern or garment so that it fits the body and represents the body measurements and proportions.

Alternate clipping: several small, straight cuts, clipping each layer of seam allowance separately to allow the seam allowances to lie flat.

Apex: bust point.

Appliqué: a cutout decoration, design or small motif that is sewn over the main fabric or garment.

Armhole: the garment opening for the arm or for the insertion of the sleeve. Another name is armscye.

Backstitch: the reverse stitch on the machine used to sew back and forth at the beginning and ending of seams to reinforce the stitching.

Bartack: short, zigzag cross stitches forming a bar to reinforce the ends of buttonholes, end of fly-zip openings, and stress points on trousers, jeans, overalls and work clothes.

Baste: long stitches used to hold fabric pieces together temporarily. Basting stitches can be made by hand or machine. Ends are not fastened or backstitched. Before stitches are removed, threads are snipped every few centimetres.

Belting: a stiff narrow band made of heavy woven material, available in various widths and weights, used as interlining and backing to reinforce waistbands and fabric-covered belts.

Bias: a line that runs diagonally across the grain of the fabric. True bias is at a 45-degree angle. Fabric cut on the true bias has the maximum stretchability of woven fabric.

Bias binding/tape: a single- or double-fold of strips cut on true bias in which one edge is stitched to the garment edges as a finish or trim.

Bias cut: cutting fabric on the bias.

Bias strip: used to finish and strengthen a raw edge. The bias strip is folded so that it encases the edge and shows on both the right and wrong sides.

Blend: yarns composed of two or more different fibres mixed together before spinning into a single yarn.

Blindstitch: a small, almost invisible hand stitch used for hemming. Slipping the needle through a fold in the cloth with each stitch conceals the thread.

Blind tucks: a number of tucks sewn so the fold of one tuck meets the stitching line of the next tuck on the inside of the garment.

Bobbin: a small round spool of thread that locks with the top thread on the machine when sewing.

Bolt: unit in which fabric is packaged by the manufacturer and sold to fabric stores.

Bonded fabric: a fabric with a tricot backing or a lightweight underlining sealed by an adhesive for added body and reinforcement.

Boning: flexible, narrow strips of featherboning or stiff nylon strip used to stiffen seams and edges of close-fitting garments (such as a strapless dress) to prevent them from slipping.

Bust dart: helps a garment fit over the bust area. Usually begins at the shoulder or side seam and finishes 5cm from the bust point (apex).

Buttonhole: a finished opening for a button, sewn either by machine or hand.

Buttonholer: attachment to make worked buttonholes of various sizes on a commercial machine.

Buttonhole twist: a thick, natural fibre silk thread used for handworked buttonholes and for other fine tailoring.

Button loop: loop made of bias tubing, thread or cord to serve as a buttonhole. They are usually placed to extend beyond the edge of the garment.

Button shank: an extension of thread, plastic or metal on the underside of a button. The shank allows the button to be held up from the fabric and to rest on top of the buttonhole.

Cable cord: soft, cotton yarn rope used for cording and tubing.

Canvas: heavy, durable cotton material made from coarse, hard-twisted yarns. Used as utility fabric and to interface fronts and other parts of coats.

Casing: a folded-over edge or an applied strip that creates a tunnel through which elastic or a drawstring or ribbon is threaded.

Catch stitch: hand-worked, short backstitches, taken alternately from left to right, ply by ply, to form a close cross stitch. Used especially for hemming.

Centre front/centre back: the line on a pattern or garment that indicates the position of the vertical centre.

Clean-finish: any method (such as zigzag stitch, overlocking or turning under) used to finish the raw edges of a garment piece, usually on hems and facings.

Clip: a small cut into the seam allowance almost to the stitchline. Used on curved seams to release strain and help the seam lie flat when turned, as on necklines or in corners of squared seams on collars, facings and necklines.

Collar: a cloth band or folded-over piece of fabric attached to the neckline of a shirt, blouse or dress.

Collar breakline: the edge of the upper lapel, folded back to make the revers.

Collar stand: the part of the collar from the crease line down to the neckline.

Crease: a line made by folding and pressing the fabric.

Crewel needle: a medium-length, oval-eyed needle used for multiple strands of thread or embroidery.

Crimping: a stitching method that slightly puckers the fabric and makes excess ease fit into the seam.

Crinoline: a coarse, stiff cotton fabric that is heavily sized; used to stiffen petticoats, to give body to contour belts and to make the headings in curtains.

Crosswise grain: threads that run across the fabric and are perpendicular to the selvedges.

Crotch seam: the part of trousers where the legs meet and a curved seam is formed.

Cuff: finish detail for the lower edge of sleeves or trousers, consisting of a separate sewn or turned-back band.

Cutting line: a long, heavy unbroken line printed on a pattern; indicates where the pattern must be cut.

Custom finish: perfection in fit, detail and construction. Usually refers to the design and make for one specific customer.

Dart: the take up of excess fabric from a specific width, tapered to nothing at one or both ends; used to aid in fitting the garment over the body curves.

Dart legs: the stitchline on both sides of the dart.

Dart point: the vanishing point and the small end of the dart.

Decorative stitching: a machine or hand embroidery stitch used for design effect.

Directional stitching: stitching in the direction of the grain to prevent the fabric from stretching. Used as a preliminary or permanent stitch.

Ease: the even distribution of slight fullness when one section of a seam is joined to a slightly shorter section without forming gathers or tucks. Used to shape set-in sleeves, princess seams and other areas.

Ease allowance: the amount added to pattern measurements to make garments more comfortable and to allow for ease of movement.

Edge stitch: to machine stitch close to a finished edge from the correct side of the fabric.

Edging: narrow, decorative border treatment of raw edges, usually using embroidery or lace, particularly on seams, hems and necklines.

Enclosed seam: a seam allowance along a faced edge that is stitched and turned to form an enclosed seam between two layers of fabric.

Fabric: a woven, knitted, felted, bonded or laminated material. Fabrics are made of both natural and synthetic fibres.

Facing: a duplicate layer of fabric stitched to a raw edge on a garment for the purpose of finishing it. It is turned to the wrong side of the garment and lies flat.

Fagotting: open thread work, used as a decorative stitch between two hemmed edges.

Felt: nonwoven fabric that is made of matted fibres of wool, fur or mohair, often mixed with cotton or rayon. Heat, moisture and pressure are applied to the fibres to form a solid mass.

Findings: term used for sewing notions or smaller items needed to make a garment, such as interfacings, zip, buttons and thread.

Finger pressing: the process of using fingers, and often steam, to press a seam that should not be flat pressed with an iron, such as a sleeve cap.

Finishing: a process to give edges of seams, facings, hems, necklines and other sections of a garment a professional look.

Flat-felled seam: a double-stitched seam. One piece is turned in and stitched on top of the first to give a finished effect on both sides of the garment.

Fly: a type of closure that conceals the zip or button openings in shorts and trousers.

Foundation garment: a finished interior garment made of heavier, supporting fabric and fitted to the body shape to hold a strapless garment in place.

Fray: small, loose threads that fall away from the cut edge of a woven fabric. Fabrics that fray easily should be edge finished.

French dart: a diagonal dart that starts at any point between the hipline and 5cm above the waist and tapers to the bust point (apex).

Gather: to draw up fabric fullness on a line of stitching.

Gathering stitch: a longer machine stitch used to draw up fullness on the stitchline.

Gimp: a fine cordlike thread used to outline a handworked buttonhole.

Give: the amount of stretch on fabric that yields to pressure without tearing or breaking.

Grade: to trim each seam allowance with an enclosed seam to varying amounts in order to reduce bulk.

Grain: sewing term that refers to the lengthwise and crosswise woven fibres of fabric.

Grainline: the lengthwise grain of fabric. On sewing patterns, the grainline is printed on a suitable straight line or edge. When placing paper pattern pieces on fabric, the grainline or arrow must lie parallel to the selvedge.

Gusset: a small fabric piece set into a slash or seam for added width and ease. Often inserted at the underarm to give ease in a sleeve.

Hand: the 'feel' of the fabric; its flexibility, smoothness and softness.

Hem: the lower edge of a garment that is finished to prevent raw edges from fraying or tearing.

Hemline: the designed line on which the hem is marked, folded, faced and turned to the underside.

Hem allowance: the extension at the bottom of skirts, dresses, blouses, sleeves and trousers, which is turned under and sewn with an appropriate hemming stitch.

Hemmer: an attachment provided with most home sewing machines to enable sewing of hems.

Hong Kong finish: the use of a narrow bias strip of fabric to conceal the raw edge of a hem or a seam.

Hook-and-loop tape: two pieces of fabric strip, with small hooks on one and a flat woolly surface on the other, which are pressed together to form a closure. Most commonly known by its trade name, Velcro.

Interfacing: fabric that is placed between a garment and facing fabric, used to add body, to give support and maintain shape.

Interlining: fabric cut into the same shape of the outer fabric and used in coats and jackets for warmth. Constructed separately and placed between the lining and the outer fabric.

Ironing: the process of smoothing and stabilizing fabric with a heated iron.

Join: in pattern direction, it usually means to stitch together the pieces using normal seam allowance and regular stitches.

Kimono sleeve: sleeve cut in one piece with the bodice front and bodice back, seamed from the shoulder down the length of the sleeve.

Lap: to fold or extend a garment piece over another.

Lapels: the front opening from the breakpoint of the garment to the turn-back of the collar.

Lengthwise grain: threads that run up and down the fabric, parallel to the selvedge.

Lining: lightweight fabric used to finish the inside of a garment. It creates a professional finish, helps to maintain the shape of the outer layer and adds warmth.

Loop turner: a rigid thin metal tool, approximately 25cm long, with a latch and hook at one end; used to turn bias tubing inside out.

Match: to bring notches or other construction markings on two pieces together.

Mercerized: cotton yarn, fabric or thread that has been finished with caustic soda to add strength and lustre to fibres and make them more receptive to dyes.

Milliner's needle: a long needle with a small rounded eye, used to make basting stitches.

Mitre: to form a diagonal seam at the square corner of a neckline or hem.

Muslin: an inexpensive, plain-woven cotton fabric made from bleached or unbleached yarns.

Muslin shell: a basic sample garment made from muslin fabric as an aid during the styling and fitting processes. Also known as a toile.

Nap: a fibrous surface produced by brushing up fibres on the fabric during the finishing process. A one-way directional pattern layout is used, with the top of all pattern pieces placed in the same direction.

Nonwoven fabric: a fabric such as interlining or felt, formed by matting together fibres through pressure and the use of heat or chemicals.

Notch: a small v-shape or clip, marking the edge of the pattern piece, which indicates those seams to be matched and not joined.

Notions: small supplies needed to make a garment, such as thread, needles, pins, buttons and zips.

Overcast seam: a seam finish made by hand with an overcasting stitch or by machine with a zigzag stitch.

Pattern markings: the symbols for darts, buttonholes, notches, dots and tucks, which are printed on patterns to guide the construction of a garment. They are transferred from the pattern to the fabric by means of tailor's tacks, notches, chalk, basting, tracing wheel or dressmaker's carbon paper.

Pick stitch: a small, durable backstitch used to hand finish a zip application. Also called hand pick stitch.

Pile: a textured fabric extending above the surface of the cloth, produced by interlacing additional looped yarns into the base, creating closely spaced loops.

Pin-basting: the use of pins to hold fabric pieces together, which can be easily removed as the fabric is stitched. Enough pins are used to keep layers from slipping.

Pin tucks: very narrow, topstitched tucks, usually about 27mm long and 3mm wide.

Pinking: the use of pinking shears to cut a serrated edge at a seam to prevent fabrics from fraying. Can also be used as a decorative edge on fabrics such as felt.

Piping: a narrow strip of cloth folded on the bias, used for trimming garments.

Pivot: to turn a square corner by leaving the needle in the fabric, lifting the presser foot and turning the fabric in another direction.

Placket: a visible overlapping strip of fabric sewn in a garment opening.

Pleat: fold of fabric, usually partially stitched, used for fitting and controlling fullness and as a garment design feature.

Ply: refers to each layer of fabric when they are laid out to be cut.

Pocket: garment detail sewn to the correct side of a garment or set into a garment seam or opening. Used for decoration and/or function.

Press: the use of an iron, with or without moisture, to flatten garment pieces and seams during construction. Pressing is a lifting and placing motion; it is not the same as ironing, which involves pushing the iron back and forth.

Presser foot: the attachment on the sewing machine that holds fabric steady while the needle is stitching. The 'all-purpose' foot is used for most stitching.

Pressure: refers to the amount of pressure the presser foot exerts on the fabric during the stitching process. The pressure can be adjusted to suit the fabric.

Quilted: two layers of fabric stitched together with a padding. Stitching may be done by hand or machine, usually in a diamond-shaped or scroll pattern.

Raw edge: the cut edge of garment pieces.

Regular stitch: permanent machine stitching. Stitch length should be adjusted according to the fabric.

Reinforce: to strengthen an area that will be subject to strain. The area may be reinforced with a stay stitch close to the stitchline or with an underlay fabric piece secured with an extra row of stitching.

Release dart: a dart that is partially stitched so that fullness is released at the end. Also called open-end dart.

Residual shrinkage: a small amount, usually five per cent, of shrinkage remaining in a finished fabric or garment. Residual shrinkage occurs gradually each time the garment is washed.

Revers: shaped lapels without a collar, used on coats, jackets, blouses and dress bodices.

Reversible: a garment that is finished so that it may be worn with either side out.

Rip: to remove stitching.

Roll: to manipulate fabric, usually along a seamline, in order to bring the seam beyond the edge to the underside of the garment.

Seam: two or more edges of fabric held together by sewing a variety of stitches. Seams should be well constructed and appropriate for the fabric, the type of garment and the location on the garment.

Seam allowance: the amount of fabric that is allocated to joining sections of a garment or other articles together.

Seam binding: a narrow, lightweight woven tape, used to cover the raw edge of a hem edge. Also used as a stay for waistline and seam reinforcement.

Seam blending: trimming all seam allowances within a seam to different widths. Blending removes bulk so that the seam will lie flat.

Seam edge: the cut edge of a seam allowance. Sometimes referred to as the raw edge.

Seam finish: the finish used on the edge of the seam allowance to prevent the fabric from fraying.

Seam guide: a device attached to the bed of the machine with clearly etched lines; used to measure seam widths.

Seamline: the line designed on patterns for stitching the seam, generally 16mm from the cut edge in home sewing and 13mm or 6mm on industrial patterns.

Seam ripper: small cutting tool used for removing unwanted stitches. Specially designed with a cutting edge and a sharp point to slip under stitched threads.

Selvedge: the narrow, firmly woven finish along the lengthwise edges of fabric.

Set-in sleeve: a sleeve with a fairly high cap that resembles the shape of the arm. Set-in sleeves are cut separately from the bodice and are stitched into the armhole after the shoulder and side seams are sewn.

Sharps needle: medium-length, all-purpose needle with a small rounded eye. Sizes range from one to 12.

Shears: a cutting tool with a blade of at least 15cm and one handle larger than the other. Larger than scissors.

Shirr: to gather up fabric on the stitchline where fullness in the garment is desired. Shirring is sometimes thought of as being multiple rows of gathers.

Shrink: to relax the fibres of fabric, usually by washing or dry cleaning, before garment construction; it prevents further shrinking.

Silk pins: fine, medium-length rustproof pins that taper to a very sharp fine point. Silk pins are less likely to leave marks on fabric.

Single knit: fabrics knit with one set of needles and one continuous yarn to form loops across the fabric width.

Sizing: a finish applied to fabrics to add body and stiffness.

Skirt/trouser darts: used to bring in the waist of a skirt or trousers. The front darts are usually shorter than the back darts.

Slash: a straight cut (longer than a clip) in the body of a garment section to make a garment opening.

Sleeve board: a small, wooden ironing board, padded with silicone-treated cotton or canvas fabric, used to press seams and sleeves.

Sleeve cap: the curved upper portion of a set-in sleeve.

Sleeve head: extra strips of soft fabric or cotton wadding inserted around the top portion of an armscye to create a smooth line and to support the roll at the sleeve cap.

Slipstitch: an invisible hand stitch used for finishing hems and facings or for joining edges of an opening. On hems and facings, the procedure is to take up one thread in the under fabric and then slip the needle in the fold of the other edge.

Snap: a pair of circular metal fasteners, with a ballpoint prong and socket, used to hold garment pieces in place.

Stay: a small piece of extra fabric or tape that is sewn to an area of the garment to reinforce and secure a position. Used at the point of a slash and at waistlines.

Staystitch: regular machine stitching applied at the stitchline before garment is assembled, used to support garment edges and prevent distortion during construction.

Stitch in the ditch: the technique of sewing a straight stitch inconspicuously in the seam well on the correct side of a previously stitched seam. The method is used to complete waistbands, cuffs, collars and French bias binding.

Stretch fabric: fabric woven with specially constructed texturized yarns to allow it to stretch when pulled, then bounce back into shape. Stretch yarns add comfort, retain shape and are wrinkle-resistant; they are often used in firmly woven denims or gabardines.

Style lines: any seamline other than shoulder seams, armhole seams or side seams. A style line usually runs from one point of a garment to another point, such as a yoke from side seam to side seam or a shoulder princess seam from shoulder to waistline.

Tack: to sew one section of a garment to another with loose, temporary stitches.

Tailoring: process of cutting, fitting and sewing a garment to conform to the body by means of darts, plackets, pockets, linings, hems and pressing.

Tailor's chalk: a small piece of chalk, approximately 4cm square with two tapered edges, used to mark lines temporarily on garment hems and other alteration points.

Tailor's ham: a firm, ham-shaped cushion used for pressing areas that require shaping. One half is covered with cotton cloth for general pressing and the other half with soft wool for pressing woollen fabric to prevent shine.

Tailor's tacks: small, temporary basting stitches of double thread sewn by hand and then cut apart. Used to mark construction symbols.

Tape measure: a narrow, firmly woven tape marked with measurements (usually metric and imperial). Metal-tipped, reversible, stretch- and shrink-proof tape measures are the most practical and accurate.

Taper: to cut fabric or sew fabric thickness, so it gradually narrows to nothing at one end.

Tension: the relationship of the needle and bobbin threads and how they interlock to form the sewing machine stitch, creating a looser or tighter stitch.

Thread: fairly thin twisted strands of yarn used for sewing.

Throat plate: a flat metal piece that sits at the base of the sewing machine just underneath the presser foot. It has a small hole through which the needle passes to the bobbin thread as it stitches. This plate also has guidelines to aid in sewing a straight seam.

Top collar: the top part of the collar visible on the finished garment.

Topstitching: one or more rows of machine stitching made on the outside of the garment through all layers of the garment. It may be close to a seamline for decorative effect or 6mm from an edge.

Tracing wheel: an instrument with a pointed or serrated circular wheel at the base, used for transferring pattern markings to fabric or pattern paper.

Tricot knit: a knit fabric created by several loops formed in a lengthwise direction.

Trim: to cut away excess fabric and make the seam narrower after the seam has been stitched. Trimming eliminates bulk and removes excess fabric in corners at any point before turning.

Trimming: different styles of braids, lace and so on, which are used as a decorative feature.

Tuck: a stitch fold, usually straight and parallel to the fold. Tucks provide relaxed but definite fullness.

Twill tape: a thin, strong cotton tape in twill weave with woven edges, used for inner construction, usually to reinforce and prevent stretching.

Underlay: a strip of fabric placed on the underside of the main garment piece; used for reinforcement on buttonholes and pockets and for decorative zigzag stitching.

Underlining: the second thickness of a carefully selected fabric that is cut in the same pattern as the garment and stitched in place with the garment seams. Used to give added body and shape. Underlining may also be strips of muslin, cut on the bias, used to underlay hems.

Understitch: to fold the entire seam allowance to the facing side or underside and stitch on the correct side of the facing close to the seam edge. This allows the seam to lie flat and keeps the seam edge from showing on the correct side of the garment.

Unit construction: a construction procedure in which each piece is sewn and pressed and kept flat for as long as possible before sleeves or collars are inserted. This reduces the amount of handling of the various pieces of a garment, which keeps them fresher looking and saves time.

Vent: a lapped opening or finished slit used in hems of tailored jackets, skirts and sleeves.

Waistband: a waistline finish. Waistbands are made with a folded-over band or a seamed, contoured piece.

Warp: the strong, lengthwise woven threads or yarns of fabric.

Wash-and-wear: term used to describe various finishes applied to fabrics. Garments made of these fabrics require little or no ironing after washing.

Weft: the crosswise woven threads or yarns of fabric.

Welt seam: a plain seam with both seam allowances pressed to one side and then held in place with one row of topstitching.

Whipstitch: a small, hand-stitched vertical seam finish, only 3mm apart, stitched over the edge of a seam.

Wide end of dart: the widest end of the dart legs.

With nap: pattern layout directive for napped fabrics, where all pattern pieces are to be placed facing the same direction.

Without nap: pattern layout direction for fabrics without a nap, where the pattern pieces may be placed in either direction.

Yoke: the fitted upper portion of a blouse, trousers or skirt.

Zigzag stitch: a regular stitch that forms a zigzag shape; all stitches are of the same width and in a straight line.

Zip: a fastening device made with metal teeth or synthetic coils that interlock to make a complete closure.

Zip foot: a single-toed presser foot that is notched on both sides to accommodate the needle and facilitate stitching close to raised edges, such as zips and cording for left or right construction.

INDEX

Page numbers in *italics* indicate illustrations.